Praise for *Chosen for Christ*

God chose us first. It's a comforting truth about our past, but it's also electric power in our present. In her book *Chosen for Christ*, Heather Holleman describes all the promise and passion bound up in the simple fact that God picked us. If you have ever struggled with feeling left out, unloved, or overlooked, this book will bring you healing, but it will also inspire you to more.

SHARON HODDE MILLER
Author of *Free of Me: Why Life Is Better When It's Not about You*

Too often we gauge our worth by our career success, relationship status, or number of "likes" on our social media posts. We desperately need a different measuring stick, and *Chosen for Christ* offers just that. With humility, vulnerability, and a serious study of Scripture, Heather Holleman shows us that God chooses us—not for some distant future greatness—but *here and now*. *Chosen for Christ* unfolds glorious potential for our ordinary days, transforming them into an extraordinary journey. This book is a resounding *YES* for anyone questioning if they are called or chosen by God.

ERICA YOUNG REITZ
Author of *After College: Navigating Transitions, Relationships and Faith*

For everyone who has felt uninvited, this book is for you. Heather writes brilliantly and beautifully showing you your status as God's chosen one. Living a chosen life will change everything about how you live your life. I highly recommend this book!

BECKY HARLING
Speaker and author of *How to Listen so People Will Talk* and *Who Do You Say That I Am?*

Our media-soaked world inundates millennials 24/7 with compelling promises of where to find their identity, purpose, and value. Problem—they are all empty, chaotic promises. There's only one place they will find contentment—in Christ. *Chosen for Christ* is a brilliant work that challenges all of us in our personal journey, as well as in our commitment to mentor next-generation leaders.

DANITA BYE
Author of *Millennials Matter: Proven Stra
Gen Leader

chosen *for Christ*

STEPPING INTO THE LIFE
YOU'VE BEEN MISSING

heather holleman

MOODY PUBLISHERS

CHICAGO

Unless otherwise noted, Scripture quotations are taken from the Holy Bible, New International Version®, NIV®. Copyright © 1973, 1978, 1984, 2011 by Biblica, Inc.™ Used by permission of Zondervan. All rights reserved worldwide. www.zondervan.com. The "NIV" and "New International Version" are trademarks registered in the United States Patent and Trademark Office by Biblica, Inc.™

Scripture passages marked ESV are from the ESV® Bible (The Holy Bible, English Standard Version®) copyright © 2001 by Crossway, a publishing ministry of Good News Publishers. Used by permission. All rights reserved.

Scripture quotations marked NLT are taken from the Holy Bible, New Living Translation, copyright ©1996, 2004, 2015 by Tyndale House Foundation. Used by permission of Tyndale House Publishers, Inc., Carol Stream, Illinois 60188. All rights reserved.

Published in association with the literary agency of D. C. Jacobson & Associates LLC, PO Box 80945, Portland, OR 97280.

Edited by Pamela J. Pugh
Author photo: BowerShots Photography
Interior design: Ragont Design
Cover design: Kelsey Fehlberg and Erik M. Peterson
Cover photo of greenhouse by Annie Spratt on Unsplash

Library of Congress Cataloging-in-Publication Data

Names: Holleman, Heather, author.
Title: Chosen for Christ : stepping into the life you've been missing /
  Heather Holleman.
Description: Chicago : Moody Publishers, 2018. | Includes bibliographical
  references.
Identifiers: LCCN 2018025690 (print) | LCCN 2018035239 (ebook) | ISBN
  9780802496485 () | ISBN 9780802416872
Subjects: LCSH: Vocation--Christianity. | Christian life.
Classification: LCC BV4740 (ebook) | LCC BV4740 .H566 2018 (print) | DDC
  248.8/43--dc23
LC record available at https://lccn.loc.gov/2018025690

ISBN: 978-0-8024-1687-2

We hope you enjoy this book from Moody Publishers. Our goal is to provide high-quality, thought-provoking books and products that connect truth to your real needs and challenges. For more information on other books and products written and produced from a biblical perspective, go to www.moodypublishers.com or write to:

Moody Publishers
820 N. LaSalle Boulevard
Chicago, IL 60610

1 3 5 7 9 10 8 6 4 2

Printed in the United States of America

For Ashley

CONTENTS

PART ONE

YOUR PRESENT
SITUATION

—⟋⟋⟋⟋—

CHAPTER I

WHEN WILL
I FEEL CHOSEN?

Who's going to want me? . . .
Whoever's going to want me? Nobody will.
—GRACE IN NICHOLAS EVANS'S *THE HORSE WHISPERER*

I roam around this snowy Pennsylvania neighborhood as the wind at my face feels like tiny teeth biting my cheeks. My teenage daughters will soon arrive home from school, and I'll welcome them with snacks of robust cheese, fresh bread, and dark chocolate while I prepare the lasagna, just like my friend—the neighborhood Italian Mama—taught me back in the days of our Italian cooking lessons. But first, I walk the streets I've now walked for ten years: past the glossy shrubs where I'll find sparrows' nests with speckled eggs in the spring, past the parking lot where I once led the neighborhood children in jump rope games, and back to the oak tree that one autumn provided enough acorns to make acorn flour for hearty bread. In a few months, the weeping cherry outside the bedroom window will bloom like pink fireworks. Then, I'll search the garden for yellow daffodils and the first signs of green leaves on the raspberry canes. *This is the life God gave me. This is the life He chose for me.*

But winter won't leave yet. And it feels like a bitter winter in my heart, too. I'm walking to calm a brewing storm inside of painful emotions that ruin the beauty of a winter walk and embarrass me with their immaturity: Once again I feel overlooked, ignored, and rejected because of an array of infractions like unavailable friends who socialize without me or how other women broadcast their writing and speaking success on social media as if to personally hurt my feelings. It's terrible. If someone else receives an honor at Penn State, I wonder why I wasn't picked. If someone else gains adoration and influence on social media, I wonder if I've squandered my time and should work harder at promoting myself so everyone will choose me to quote and to headline as their keynote speaker.

I don't want to feel this way anymore. It's killing me inside.

But these thoughts feel so familiar they arrive like regular guests in my heart. I think back to all those times I wanted to be chosen for something or someone—a boy, an award, a school, a sorority, a job, a book contract. The list goes on. Even into adulthood, my heart jumps up and down like a rambunctious first-grader screaming, "Pick me! Pick me! Pick me!" And I'm that little girl Grace in the novel *The Horse Whisperer* who, even after undergoing a partial amputation of her leg, has only *one concern*. She cries out to her mother as she sobs on her bed, "Who's going to want me? . . . Whoever's going to want me? Nobody will."[1]

> *Jesus, heal this ache in me. When*
> *will I stop wanting to feel chosen?*

I slow my walk and consider the truth: The feeling of needing someone to choose us doesn't go away—even after we find our marriage partner, our job, or any other person or experience we think will soothe this inescapable need. We shape our identity on how chosen we feel at any given time, both by people and for opportunities. As one of the deepest and sustained longings of the human heart, the need to feel chosen drives us to arrange our whole lives to chase that chosen feeling that might depart at times but always returns into our hearts as predictably as the seasons.

As I walked home on that snowy day, I remembered these words from Jesus as He speaks in John 15:16: ". . . I chose you and appointed you so that you might go and bear fruit—fruit that will last . . ."

I chose you.

I chose you and appointed you to bear fruit.

As the snow fell in soft flakes, I knew that if God taught me more about my chosen identity, it could offer the remedy for past, present, and even future rejection. It would also provide certainty that God chose me for this exact life I'm living—to bear the fruit He appointed for me.

—⁂—

Can you imagine firmly settling in your mind that you've been chosen for Someone and that each new day you will step into a life chosen for you? Imagine the intimacy with Jesus available to you. Imagine the joy and peace of living a chosen life.

God *chooses* us—described most clearly in Ephesians 1:3–13 where the apostle Paul writes to help Christians understand their identity in Christ. I had spent years studying chapter 2 of Ephesians and learning about my "seated" identity (2:6) that prompted the book *Seated with Christ*, but I somehow overlooked an even deeper and primary need of my heart in the chapter before: living as *chosen*. Knowing I was seated with Christ solved the problem of jealousy and comparison, and now this new word—chosen—promised to repair an enduring fear of rejection from both people and opportunities. I could live in the reality of having already been chosen by the One my heart most wants.

Paul writes in Ephesians 1 that we are blessed "in the heavenly realms with every spiritual blessing" (v. 3). He insists that God "chose us in him before the creation of the world" and that He "predestined us for adoption" (vv. 4–5). Paul reminds us once more that "in him we were also chosen . . . according to the plan of him who works out everything in conformity with the purpose of his will" (v. 11).

Paul tells me I'm chosen and in John 15:16, Jesus tells me I'm chosen: "You did not choose me, but I chose you and appointed you so that you might go and bear fruit—fruit that will last—and so that whatever you ask in my name the Father will give you."

Even Peter tells me I'm part of a "chosen people" as he writes in 1 Peter 2:9, "But you are a chosen people, a royal priesthood, a holy nation, God's special possession, that you may declare the praises of him who called you out of darkness into his wonderful light." Just like Jesus, we are, as Peter writes, "rejected by humans but chosen by God and precious to him" (1 Peter 2:4b).

The Old Testament, too, announces repeatedly that God chooses people to be His treasured possession.[2]

This past year, I explored the single verb in Scripture—that God *chose* you and me—and I arrived at the life-changing conclusion that God not only chooses us personally for Jesus—we have, Scripture says, been "given" to Jesus (John 17:24)—but He also arranges the opportunities and fruitfulness of our lives. Yet our chosen identity extends far beyond belonging and bearing fruit for God's kingdom. In fact, by examining this theologically rich verb in Scripture, I uncovered seven reasons why God chooses us that transformed my life. I'll share these reasons—which are His invitations to you—throughout this book, and I pray you'll experience the same profound realization that I did:

LIVE AS ONE *CHOSEN*—CHOSEN FOR AN EXTRAORDINARY GOD WHO INVITES US TO LIVE AN EXTRAORDINARY LIFE.

I need no longer live in rejection. I need no longer live in confusion about my calling.

I live as one *chosen*—chosen for Christ and His purposes. The verb became a stake in the ground, a solid marker that right here in my life I'm chosen for an extraordinary God who invites me to live an extraordinary life.

The word *chosen* serves as the balm for the ache of longing I feel in my own heart and learn about through the lives of thousands of young adults, college students, and professionals I've encountered in nearly two decades of college teaching and adult ministry. And I assume this might resonate with your own heart today:

I'm tired of being ignored, passed over, and uncertain of my future. I'm mocked by my collection of rejection letters, of wedding invitations to everyone else's fairy tale, of promotions not granted, and prizes never awarded. It's always the other girl chosen, not me. Now I'm growing older and accumulating more and more rejection and uncertainty. If only I were chosen every once in a while. How different life would feel if someone chose me, if I were the special, favored one just once in my ordinary life!

Maybe you also feel like I once did in my mid-forties: maybe you did find a marriage partner and some measure of career success, but you still feel the same old ache. Before realizing my chosen identity, I often lived with a disorienting feeling that I didn't know exactly what I was supposed to be doing. *Did God really choose me for this life, in this career, with these people? How far does His choosing work extend? And why am I still waiting to feel chosen?*

Unsure of God's choosing of my circumstances, and unable to fathom His loving, personal choosing of me for Jesus, I was waiting to be chosen for the next important opportunity that would bring significance and certainty to my life.

You know the feeling, right? You want a clear plan, grand goals, and a sense of a personal mission. Maybe, like me, you've been raised on the language of purpose, achievement, and calling. And now you worry you've missed something.

You feel confusion and dread instead of clarity and peace.

If you live with any degree of confusion, fear, or a sense of rejection that pollutes your life, we have more in common than you think.

It's a terrible way to live when you fight to be *chosen*. It poisons you. And it poisons your soul to think that you aren't living the life you're *chosen to live*, as if God made a cosmic blunder when it came to managing you.

> IT POISONS YOUR SOUL TO THINK THAT YOU AREN'T LIVING THE LIFE YOU'RE *CHOSEN TO LIVE*, AS IF GOD MADE A COSMIC BLUNDER WHEN IT CAME TO MANAGING YOU.

Isn't there a better way to live? Is there anything in Scripture to heal us of this ancient need, this all-consuming longing? What does God tell us?

—⟶⟵—

An apostle of Jesus Christ named Peter writes to scattered, uncertain, and discouraged Christians to remember their identity and their calling. Peter knows about a chosen life. Peter's the kind of man so passionate about Jesus that when he sees Jesus on the shore from where he sat in his fishing boat, he "threw himself into the sea" to swim to Jesus (John 21:7b ESV). If you follow Peter's life in the book of Acts, you'll read of how God empowered his speaking and performed incredible miracles through him, like healing a man unable to walk and raising a woman from the dead. God also speaks to Peter in a special vision and sends an angel to rescue him from prison. People were so amazed by God's work through Peter that they brought their sick near him "so that at least Peter's shadow might fall on some of them" (Acts 5:15).

Peter knew Jesus, loved Jesus, and served Jesus in supernatural ways. This ordinary fisherman declares this:

> But you are a chosen people, a royal priesthood, a holy nation, God's special possession, that you may declare the praises of him who called you out of darkness into his wonderful light. (1 Peter 2:9)

You are—along with others—chosen, royal, holy, God's special possession. You live in His wonderful light.

I read these words from my worn green Bible as I sit in the mustard recliner by the window. The weeping cherry, stark and icy, stretches out dark, curled fingers of branches. I'm praying that Peter's words sink in deeply as I look more carefully at the passage.

As a college writing instructor and lover of verbs, I immediately note the present tense description of God's people—that includes you and me—as *currently* chosen, royal, holy, and special.

This isn't something that's going to happen to us in a heavenly future; it's happening *now*. Peter doesn't say, "You *will be* a chosen people"—he says, "You *are* a chosen people."

These verses teach we are chosen, royal, and God's special possession. We are chosen to live in the presence of God and declare how He saved us from darkness. If you were to look for other references to our chosen identity, you would find Paul writing this in Ephesians 1:11 (ESV): We are chosen "according to the purpose of him who works all things according to the counsel of his will." God, therefore, chooses us and works out *all things* in our lives according to His good and loving plans. Before we learn anything else about why God chooses us, it matters most of all that we understand God as not only declaring our identity as His special, chosen possession, but also as a God working out the details of our lives.

This twofold understanding of our chosen identity—as called to belong to a loving God and to the life He has designed for us—answers the predictable cry of our heart to feel chosen and also anchors us when life feels confusing and painful. We can declare this:

He chose me. I belong to God. I am precious to Him. Because God brings everything in my life under His control, I trust that I'm chosen for this life, in this place, with these people, at this time in history, with work God ordains for me and enables me to do by the power of the Holy Spirit.

As I wondered about our chosen identity, I began to ask *why* God chose me. Is it for my perfect life plan to work out? In Colossians 1:16b, we read, "all things have been created through him and for him." Was I created *for* Jesus? If so, what if, instead of longing to be chosen for certain external things—people, places, and professions—we realize we're chosen to belong to Jesus for His purposes, not our own? What happens when we believe we are chosen for Christ and not for ourselves? And what if the point of today isn't our plan but rather to respond to the seven reasons God chose us for Christ?

This means we're chosen for a Person, not a perfect life plan.

Now, instead of finding the perfect calling, a personal mission, and a fulfilling life, we might search the Scriptures to learn more about how God invites us to live. In fact, by doing so, we find a set of governing principles that revolutionizes how we experience daily life. Your life plan assumes secondary importance; it comes as a byproduct of living as God intends. Your mission and vision will naturally overflow as you abide with Jesus as His chosen one.

As I explored that little verb *chose*, I discovered that the reasons why God chooses us have very little—if not nothing at all—to do with personal impact and career success. The reasons God chooses us orchestrate a biblical purpose for living that begins with living radically different lives that exalt Jesus Christ. Chosen people step into abundant life because of Jesus. We step into the life we've been missing all this time . . . because of Jesus.

The life you've been missing starts today.

GOD'S INVITATION TO YOU

—⟋⟍⟍—

Each new day let's see our circumstances as invitations to seven biblical purposes that we are going to explore together. God's invitations to His chosen people include:

Worship—1 Peter 2:9

Live as God's Treasured Possession—Deuteronomy 14:2b

Belong to a New Family—Ephesians 2:19

Complete Good Works—John 15:16

Display God's Power—Psalm 65:5

Become Like Jesus—Romans 8:29

Live Differently from the World—Romans 12:2

I think about my day so differently as a chosen woman; I look at circumstances and understand them as opportunities to experience the Christian life in these seven ways. And now, the same Pennsylvanian neighborhood walk, the same march across Penn State's campus, swinging my blue striped bag and sloshing my coffee, to arrive to my advanced writing classes, and the same ordinary rhythms of family life of baking and housecleaning mean something so different. It's a life of knowing to whom I belong and why I'm here.

Living a chosen life sets us free from the need to find validation anywhere else but in God—even when everyone else gains attention or awards. We don't need anyone else or any experience to make us feel special or valued. And we're set free to settle into our lives because we believe God chose us for the life we're living.

And now, we take the first step into this chosen life.

YOUR NEXT STEP

—ന്ന—

Read Ephesians 1:1–14 and 1 Peter 2:9–10.

1. When you read the above passages, what images and emotions come to mind when you think of God choosing you to belong to Him?

2. As you analyze the current state of your heart, fill in the blank. "I would feel chosen and special if _____ (this person) or _____(this school /employer / group / award committee / publisher, etc.) chose me."

3. What would change about your daily experience if you believed God chose you for Christ and for the life He's given you?

4. Begin thinking what it could mean to be chosen for a Person (Jesus Christ!), not a plan. What does that mean to you?

CHAPTER 2

THIS LIFE NOW

"From one man he made all the nations, that they should inhabit the whole earth; and he marked out their appointed times in history and the boundaries of their lands. God did this so that they would seek him and perhaps reach out for him and find him, though he is not far from any one of us."

—PAUL SPEAKING IN ACTS 17:26–27

You don't have to wait to experience a chosen life. Where do you live? Think about your home, the people around you, and your schedule for today. Now, believe God chose you for Christ and for this life you're living. It's not an accident, a mistake, or beyond the sovereign choice of God to position you where you are.

It took me most of my adult life to believe this. And when I battled six years of clinical depression after my life plans fell apart, I wondered how it could be true that God chose me for this life.

You might look at those seven invitations to a different way of living and think: "Nobody knows my life. Nobody knows how hard and frustrating it is. There's no way I can live as being chosen when God seems to have chosen me for a miserable life."

But what if you could?

What if you began to believe that God didn't make a mistake? What if you believed He intends to show you His power and love right where you are, maybe even *because* of where you are? More importantly, will you accept God's governing rule in your life? Will you agree to live the life He asks you to live and respond in worship?

In order to believe that, despite what's happening to us, God offers these invitations to us as His chosen children, we must first believe that God chooses to allow the circumstances of our lives. Nothing happening to you as a Christ follower is happening on accident or by mistake. Nothing happening to you is beyond the sovereign choice of God to allow it. We serve a God who works out *every detail of our lives*. The promise of Romans 8:28 stands as one of the most beautiful but difficult passages to believe. It reads: "And we know that in all things God works for the good of those who love him, who have been called according to his purpose." God is working for our good in "all things." He doesn't miss anything about our lives. He sees everything going on with you and is already working to bring good out of what's happening to you, even if you are in the midst of unspeakable pain and brokenness right now.

In fact, Jesus explains to His disciples what it means to live without fear and to trust in God's care for their lives. He says in Matthew 10:29–31: "Are not two sparrows sold for a penny? Yet not one of them will fall to the ground outside your Father's care. And even the very hairs of your head are all numbered. So don't be afraid; you are worth more than many sparrows." I watch the tiny sparrows outside the window and think about not even one of them falling to the ground outside of God's care.

WHAT IF, THIS VERY DAY, YOU ALLOWED YOURSELF TO BELIEVE THAT GOD HOLDS YOUR LIFE—AND ALL YOUR WAYS—IN HIS HANDS?

Is anything outside of God's providential care? Is there anything about us He doesn't know or understand, even each strand of hair? Consider Psalm 33:15, where the writer proclaims that God "forms the hearts of all [and] considers everything they do."

Everything. God considers everything you do.

God knows about the bills you must pay, the medical results you're waiting for, and the relationship strain you might be experiencing. He knows about that upcoming test, the interview scheduled, and the people you're about to meet.

In the Bible Daniel tells us something profound about God when he describes Him as the One "who holds in his hand your life and all your ways" (Dan. 5:23b). What if, this very day, you allowed yourself to believe that God holds your life—and all your ways—in His hands?

He knows you. He sees you. He holds everything about your life in His hands.

International Bible teacher Kay Arthur, in *Lord, I Want to Know You*, presents one of the Hebrew names of God, El Elyon, which means the "sovereign ruler of all the universe." She asks, "What difference does it make in your life to realize that God is sovereign, that He is ruler over all and that nothing can happen without the ultimate sanction or permission of God?"[1]

I felt myself exhale when I read that, as if all the pent-up anxiety and dread had dissolved. *God was working right here in the circumstances in my life that He has sovereignly allowed.* I wanted to learn more and more about trusting God's sovereignty, so I collected the words of great heroes of the Christian faith, like Holocaust survivor Corrie ten Boom, who wrote: "Every experience God gives us, every person He puts in our lives is the perfect preparation for the future that only He can see."[2]

I may not see the future, but He does. I may feel unsure, but as Os Guinness says, we can be "unsure of ourselves" but "sure of God."[3] I'm sure of God. I'm sure that He is in control of what might feel out of control in my life.

I'm God's *chosen child*, and He not only chooses me for Himself, but He's a good and loving God who delights in my well-being and works out everything to conform to His purposes. He's a God who chooses the circumstances of my life—no matter how bitter and bleak—for His glory and my good as I allow Him to transform these places.

—⁄⁄⁄—

What would help us believe that God chose us *for Himself,* but that He also chooses *the circumstances of our lives* for particularly glorious reasons? What if we believed, like never before in our lives, that God orders our lives according to His divine choosing? What if we believed that God governs all things in our lives, that nothing exists outside of His power and dominion, and that everything happening to us works to reveal something about Jesus, to bring us deeper into the life of Christ, and to allow us to live the life for which we were designed as chosen people?

WHAT IF WE BELIEVED THAT GOD GOVERNS ALL THINGS IN OUR LIVES . . . TO ALLOW US TO LIVE THE LIFE FOR WHICH WE WERE DESIGNED AS CHOSEN PEOPLE?

Consider the following verses that prime our souls to step into the life we've been missing due to the confusion and fear we have about our lives. To receive the seven invitations to this supernatural chosen life—that happens right where you live in the very circumstances you might struggle with about your life—we start with four core beliefs:

1. *God determines where we live.* In Acts 17:26, Paul declares, "From one man he made all the nations, that they should inhabit the whole earth; and he marked out their appointed times in history and the boundaries of their lands." In the ESV translation, it reads that God set "the boundaries of their dwelling place." In the 1984 version of the NIV, we read that God "determined the times set for them and the *exact places* where they should live" (emphasis mine). Can you imagine believing right now that God chose you for your home and the time you are living there? He did this for a special purpose that we learn about in the next verse: "And God did this so that [we] would seek him and perhaps reach out for him and find him, though he is not far from any one of us" (v. 27). God chooses where you live and when you live there as a way of encouraging your seeking and finding of Jesus.

2. *God chooses the fruit of our lives.* In Ephesians 2:10 Paul explains that we are "created in Christ Jesus to do good works, which God prepared in advance for us to do." God designs the good works for our lives. Jesus tells us clearly in John 15:16–17a this truth: "You did not choose me, but I chose you and appointed you that you might go and bear fruit—fruit that will last . . ." We finally learn in Philippians 2:13 that "it is God who works in [us] to will and to act in order to fulfill his good purpose." As you look at your day, imagine it stretching out before you with good works prepared in advance that God will give you the desire and the power to complete. As I pray about God choosing me to bear fruit, I go about my chores and my professional life with a joyous, adventurous

expectancy that God might use me for good works—as an agent of blessing and proclamation—wherever I go. In fact, He ordains the where, how, what, and when of the good works prepared for us. We might look around the boundaries of our day and consider it as the right soil we need to bear the fruit designed for us.

3. *God will lead us in His plans for our future.* I take great comfort in the beautiful promise in Isaiah 48:17: "This is what the LORD says—your Redeemer, the Holy One of Israel: 'I am the LORD your God, who teaches you what is best for you, who directs you in the way you should go.'" When I was most confused about my calling (What am I doing in graduate school?), sense of place (Why am I living here? I don't like it!), and community (I feel so lonely!), God comforted me deeply with this verse in Psalm 57:2 (ESV): "I cry out to the God Most High, to God who fulfills his purpose for me." To name the Lord the *God Most High* indicates His complete control and dominion over the universe. Nothing is outside of His dominion, including you and your future. He *will* fulfill His purpose for you. He will! Finally, you can rest in the promise of Philippians 1:6 that "he who began a good work in you will carry it on to completion until the day of Christ Jesus."

4. *God is always working to bring good to us through the circumstances of our lives.* In Genesis 50:20 Joseph tells us something about God's character. Joseph tells the very people who sold him into slavery in Egypt this: "You intended to harm me, but God intended it for good to accomplish what is now being done, the saving of many lives." We remember Romans 8:28—that God works *all things* for good in our lives—but also the words of the prophet Isaiah, who proclaims that our God acts on our behalf

(Isa. 64:4) and Jeremiah, who says that God *never stops* doing good to us (Jer. 32:40).

—⁓⁓—

In response to these four truths—that God ordains where and when I live, chooses the fruit of my life, instructs me in my calling, and always works through my circumstances to bring about good—I settle down into my life with a new security, peace, and joy. Now life runs according to these fixed spiritual principles of God's governing care, not my physical circumstances including time, money, health, or any other resource.

I walk around the boundaries of this ordinary day in an ordinary neighborhood, rejoicing because of Jesus choosing me for Himself and for this very life. How can life feel so wonderful, so bursting at the seams with possibility and so set free from earthly limitations? How can this regular life—with all the failures of what it means to be human—elevate to the level of sublime holiness and indescribable joy?

It's because we're chosen for Christ and for this life He's given us.

YOUR NEXT STEP

—⁓⁓—

Read Romans 8:28 and Isaiah 48:17.

1. What does it mean to you that God is El Elyon, the Sovereign Ruler of the universe, and that nothing happens to you without His permission?

2. What's happening in your life right now that tempts you to believe you are not God's precious and chosen child?

3. What past or present evidence do you have that God ordains *where you live*, chooses *the fruit of your life*, instructs you in *your calling*, and always works through *your circumstances* to bring about good?

4. How has God directed you where you should go so far in your life?

CHAPTER 3

—ᚙᚙ—

THE BEST QUESTION

"But what about you?" he asked. "Who do you say I am?"
—JESUS SPEAKING TO SIMON PETER (MATTHEW 16:15)

As a nineteen-year-old college student, I lived with a gnawing, condemning fear that *I wasn't chosen by God*. It's a horrible way to live. Maybe God had chosen me at one point as a young girl, but now He surely changed His mind and rejected me forever. I didn't understand anything about what the Bible taught on how and why God chooses people. I worried over concepts I couldn't understand like *predestination* and *election*. Crying in my apartment at the University of Virginia on the flowered Laura Ashley bedspread, I begged God to choose me. I felt dirty and broken inside. I felt so far from Him and was sure He had rejected me forever. I asked, "Why don't I feel chosen? What if I never feel chosen?"

I wish I'd known how to ask a better question—the best question a person can ask herself. I wish I pictured Jesus asking me what He asks Simon Peter in Matthew 16:15.

Jesus asks, "Who do you say I am?"

Simon Peter answers, "You are the Messiah, the Son of the living God" (v. 16) and Jesus replies, "Blessed are you, Simon son of Jonah, for this was not revealed to you by flesh and blood, but by my Father in heaven" (v. 17).

If Jesus asked you the same question[1] He asked Peter—the

most important question you will ever answer in your entire life—
what would you say?

What I wish I knew then—that God has so clearly taught me
now—is how, instead of relying on my emotions or trying to understand how God chooses people, I now rest in the finished work
of Jesus on the cross and the reality that I stand forgiven of my sins
and now live firmly established in the chosen family of God.

If Jesus had asked me, the answer would have been so easy, so
clear. I would have answered that I believe in Jesus as the one, true
God who made a provision for our sin through His death on the
cross. We would remember together my decision—a conscious declaration of my will—to receive the free gift of salvation as a twelve-
year-old. I would have told Jesus that I had said what Paul told me to
do in Romans 10:9, which states so succinctly, "If you declare with
your mouth, 'Jesus is Lord,' and believe in your heart that God raised
him from the dead, you will be saved." Or I could have pleaded the
truth of 1 John 5:11–12: "And this is the testimony: God has given
us eternal life, and this life is in his Son. Whoever has the Son has
life; whoever does not have the Son of God does not have life."

I knew I had the Son of God because I asked Jesus to be my Lord
and Savior. I declared this in a public baptism. I gave Jesus full permission to come into my life and take over every part of it. I accepted
His blood sacrifice for sin—by His death on the cross—as payment
for my sin. I confessed I was a sinner and asked for God's forgiveness.

But back in that college apartment, I didn't imagine Jesus asking me that question He asked Simon Peter. Instead, I continued to
cry on my bed in the darkness, whimpering like a wounded dog. I
didn't *feel* like a chosen daughter of God, even though I had prayed
a prayer of salvation and was even baptized at church. I felt like
I had walked too far away from God. I had sinned against Him

too much while a Christian—mostly involving drinking and compromising in my dating life. Maybe you feel this way, and you're reading this book as someone coming home to the Lord after many years of living destructively. Maybe you don't believe God would ever choose you because you've disobeyed His commands for too long. I can relate. When I returned to God in prayer and confession, I never felt His love in my heart that year. Instead, I felt condemnation and silence.

My sister knew I was experiencing a profound spiritual struggle and had no peace in my life regarding Jesus. She wrote me letters with Bible verses written on notecards with flower stickers for me to put on my mirror. When the sorority rejected me in my freshman year while every other friend danced and cheered about their invitations from their new "sisters," my sister sent me a bouquet of flowers. She wrote on the card tucked in the flowers, "From your real big sister."

Sitting in a coffee shop with my sister who I knew loved Jesus, I sobbed and said, "Jesus would never choose me! I'm not chosen!" She calmly reminded me that the choosing was already accomplished; it didn't matter how I felt about it or whether I perceived it in some romantic, emotional way. It might quite simply be a matter of *repentance*, of turning away from sin and back to living a life that honors God in every area.

Again, I said, "But the Bible says we're a bride of Christ, but Jesus would never pick me as His bride!" I pictured a row of beautiful brides in gorgeous gowns and Jesus passing me by. I would never be the kind of woman Jesus would want. I kept weeping because *I didn't feel chosen.*

The memory burns in my mind.

Do you feel this way? Or do you know someone else who does?

Now, twenty years later, I reposition these new burgundy glasses that will transition to bifocals next year, and I'm eagerly telling a friend about seven reasons God chooses her and this new life God invites her to step into today. I'm drinking coffee now with weathered hands beginning to wrinkle and show blue veins. I'm not that young girl in the coffee shop anymore who feels like she destroyed her life. Instead, I'm filled with awe about this chosen life. I can't stop talking about it. I know I'm chosen, and I'm learning how chosen people actually live.

I prepare myself for the question I know will come. I know my friend is going to ask one of two questions:

She may immediately dig around in her purse for a notebook and pen and ask with an eager and joyful heart, "What are the seven reasons? I need those reasons!"

Or she's the woman who leans in and whispers: "But wait. What if I don't feel chosen?"

What if I don't feel chosen?

My mind goes back to the coffee shop. I remember the pain.

One woman approached me with intensity, confusion, and fear. Her wide eyes narrowed as she listened patiently while I described what God was teaching me in the Bible about a new way to live as a chosen woman. She interrupted me and grabbed my arm. "What if I don't feel chosen? I don't feel chosen. I've been to church all my life. I read my Bible. I don't feel that God chose me. What if I don't feel chosen?"

Before I could answer, she asked, "Would you write a section in your book called *What if I Don't Feel Chosen?*"

As I spoke to this woman and other people about this feeling of "not being chosen by God"—an emotion clearly part of my own spiritual journey—I probed more into their lives. They might feel as if they live blessed lives, and they might even attend church, read their Bibles, pray, and have been raised in the Christian faith. Yet they feel in their hearts that God is silent and indifferent. They don't *feel* chosen or treasured. They don't feel any personal connection to God at all. They might even say in despair, "I'm just not one of the elect. I'm not one of God's chosen ones." They might even use words like predestination and claim that God has not predestined them for salvation. Or they worry other people they know aren't chosen by God. How would anyone really know if they were chosen? What would it feel like? What would life look like then?

I can tell these friends what Jesus began to teach me from that moment in the coffee shop until this very day. Back then I didn't understand how to trust the Scriptures; I only knew I *felt* rejection. I had come to Jesus so earnestly without realizing that Jesus says, "Whoever comes to me I will never drive away" (John 6:37). When I struggled with whether or not God had chosen me as His daughter, I could have easily recited John 1:12: "Yet to all who did receive him, to those who believed in his name, he gave the right to become children of God" and the beautiful truth of John 10:28 that no one can snatch us out of God's hand. Finally, I might have recalled Jesus saying this in John 5:24: "Whoever hears my word and believes him who sent me has eternal life and will not be judged but has crossed over from death to life."

I studied these passages and underlined them in blue ink and then highlighted them in my Bible. I stayed tucked underneath that Laura Ashley bedspread with a reading lamp curved over my head in the darkness. I kept meeting with Jesus through the words on the page.

And, miraculously, I began to believe them.

I recited Romans 8:1 over and over again for months: "Therefore, there is now no condemnation for those who are in Christ Jesus." I declared—by faith and because of the truth of God's Word, not because of my feelings—that I was a child of God, chosen and beloved. I announced these truths to my own heart, day after day, whether my emotions confirmed these truths or not. Then I discovered the truth of Romans 8:16: "The Spirit himself testifies with our spirit that we are God's children." I prayed that the Holy Spirit would indeed testify, in a way I could understand, so I would know I was a child of God.

In my spirit I came to know the truth: I belonged to God.

I was His chosen child.

I pray for this confirmation in your own heart.

In simple terms, I invite my friends to ask a better question to move them into lives of faith despite their feelings: *Who do you say Jesus is? What would it mean for you to trust the Scriptures and not base your experience of being chosen on your emotions?*

On days when I don't feel like God's chosen daughter, I go back to the Scriptures that confirm the truth. I tell God I don't feel chosen. I confess any sin that contributes to feeling out of fellowship with God. If you still feel distant from God, remember that nothing can separate you from God's love (not even you) as declared in these ringing words of Romans 8:38–39: "For I am convinced that neither death nor life, neither angels nor demons, neither the present nor the future, nor any powers, neither height

IF YOU STILL FEEL DISTANT FROM GOD, REMEMBER THAT NOTHING CAN SEPARATE YOU FROM GOD'S LOVE (NOT EVEN YOU).

nor depth, nor anything else in all creation, will be able to separate us from the love of God that is in Christ Jesus our Lord."

And remember you aren't alone. Paul's most powerful prayer for the believers at Ephesus was that God would give them a "Spirit of wisdom and revelation" (Eph. 1:17) to know God and that "the eyes of [their] heart may be enlightened" to understand the hope, riches, and power they have as Christ's chosen child (1:18–19).

I pray this for you reading this right now. I pray that you would know the truth:

You are chosen.

You are His.

As I stood there with my friend who didn't feel chosen, I thought about asking this question:

"What would it take for you to feel as if you belong to Jesus?"

I imagine Jesus asking us the same question in our doubt. We've become His children, and nothing can ever change the fact that we've become alive in Him. This spiritual reality makes us permanently sealed by the Holy Spirit, and it's as certified as what a DNA test would reveal about a biological child. Ephesians 1:13 promises us,

WHAT WOULD IT TAKE FOR YOU TO FEEL AS IF YOU BELONG TO JESUS?

> And you also were included in Christ when you heard the message of truth, the gospel of your salvation. When you believed, you were marked in him with a seal, the promised Holy Spirit.

And just like a birth certificate that shows your name and the truth of your belonging to your father, our names are written in the Lamb's book of life (Rev. 21:27).

What would it take for you to know you are God's chosen child and that you belong to Jesus? Instead of living in doubt, chosen men and women live confident in their relationship with Christ.

Your chosen life begins with stepping out in certainty. You are chosen.

YOUR NEXT STEP

Read John 3:1–21, Romans 10:9–13, and 1 John 5:1–12.

1. The verses above talk about how we become a child of God. Write out your memory of asking Jesus to forgive your sins and become your Lord and Savior. When did that happen?

   If it hasn't happened yet, now is the time! You can record the day and time below. You can pray something like this: *Jesus, I know I'm a sinner who needs to receive forgiveness. Thank You for dying on the cross to pay the penalty of my sin and to put me back into a right relationship with God. I now receive Your free gift of salvation. I ask You to come into my life, forgive my sin, and make me into the person You want me to be. I place my life into Your keeping. Thank You for making me a child of God today.*

2. Do you feel certain of your own salvation? What helped you to gain this certainty?

3. What would you tell a friend who had prayed to receive Christ but still did not feel chosen?

4. If someone came to you and asked how to become a Christian, what would you tell them?

CHAPTER 4

---m---

FOR A PERSON,
NOT A PLAN

I began to live as if there were nothing,
absolutely nothing but Him.

—BROTHER LAWRENCE IN
THE PRACTICE OF THE PRESENCE OF GOD

"Return, faithless people," declares the LORD, "for I am
your husband. I will choose you—one from a town
and two from a clan—and bring you to Zion."

—JEREMIAH 3:14

My daughters and I have watched nearly every episode of *Say Yes to the Dress*. I'll admit to you now, if Pinterest had existed when I was a girl, I would have planned my wedding with as much specificity as my college students do. The seniors in my class at Penn State recently explained to me that every woman they know has their wedding planned on Pinterest—down to the type of proposal setting (a field of wildflowers or a mountainside), the location (garden and then a barn reception), the favors (personalized Mason jar candles), and the send-off (white sparklers, no rice).

I've been thinking about brides for a while now—not just

because of a television show or college students with elaborate wedding plans—but because of something unusual I noticed in Scripture. I wanted to know *why* God chose me, and I found myself so captivated by the tiniest word in Colossians 1:15–17. Here we read something astonishing and often overlooked about Jesus Christ. Paul writes,

> The Son is the image of the invisible God, the firstborn over all creation. For in him all things were created: things in heaven and on earth, visible and invisible, whether thrones or powers or rulers or authorities; all things have been created through him and for him. He is before all things, and in him all things hold together.

I love reading these words about Jesus who is the "image of the invisible God." He's the Lord; He's the creator; He's the owner of the universe; He's the one holding all things together. But did you notice that little preposition?

For.

All things have been created through Jesus and *FOR* Jesus.

—⟋⟍—

If you explore this tiny word in the original Greek language, existing "for" Him means we "answer to His purposes" as the "final cause" for why we exist.[1] The idea that we are chosen for Jesus means that everything about our lives ultimately serves His loving and good purposes. Jesus describes us in His final prayer to His Father for future believers in John 17:24 as "those you have given me." We exist *for* Him.

God has given us to Jesus.

That's when I thought of a bride, a bride *given away* to Jesus.

I think about being formed, chosen, and given for Christ—to both belong to Him and to serve His purposes—as the sole reason for my existence, my raison d'être, the final explanation of why I'm here and for whom. Scripture teaches that the church—you and I and the family of believers—becomes the *bride of Christ*, and understanding the love relationship in marriage unlocks a deeper understanding about what it means that we were created for a love relationship with Jesus. We're made for Him, to experience this love.

This means I'm chosen for a Person, not a *plan*. I'm chosen for a Living Christ, not some vague idea or philosophy. Knowing I'm chosen for a Person allows me to relax when I'm unsure of God's plan for my life.

—◊◊◊—

The prophet Isaiah declares, "As a bridegroom rejoices over his bride, so will your God rejoice over you" (Isa. 62:5). In Revelation 21:2 John describes the church as a "bride beautifully dressed for her husband." In Psalm 45 we see a stunning prophecy about Christ and His bride where the beauty of a bride—who comes to wed this majestic and mighty ruler—completely enthralls this King. This loving King says, "I have loved you with an everlasting love; I have drawn you with unfailing kindness" (Jer. 31:3). Our chosen identity has everything to do with us experiencing this everlasting love and unfailing kindness. Paul even prays in Ephesians 3 that we would "grasp how wide and long and high and deep is the love of Christ, and to know this love that surpasses knowledge" (18b–19a). This love makes John passionately exclaim in 1 John 3:1, "See what great love the Father has lavished on us, that we should be called children of God! And that is what we are!"

Seeing ourselves as the bride of Christ—adored, treasured, attended to, and celebrated—helps us understand this lavish love and inhabit our chosen status as belonging to Jesus.

Jesus made me for Him—to enjoy this love while embracing all the reasons God chose me for Christ—not for any other goal I might have. I serve the purposes of Christ as I worship, live as God's treasured possession, belong to a new family, complete the good works He's planned for me, display God's power, become more like Him, and live differently from the world. When I live like this, I exalt the name of Jesus more and more. I showcase who He is and how He's working in the world.

This chosen life changes everything about the focus on my day. I think about Jesus—and my status as existing for Him—all day long. And in case you're wondering if God specifically thinks of you this way, and not only in a collective form of the church as a whole, let me encourage you with a few truths from Scripture. In other words, you may ask, "Did God really make me and choose me specifically, or am I part of some larger population—like when God chose the entire nation of Israel as His treasured possession? How specific is this choosing?"

If you examine the number of times in Scripture God says that He chooses people "by name," your heart will warm to Jesus. This is a God who says to Jeremiah, "Before I formed you in the womb I knew you, before you were born I set you apart" (Jer. 1:5a). This is a God David worships by saying, "For you created my inmost being; you knit me together in my mother's womb. . . . Your eyes saw my unformed body. All the days ordained for me were written in your book before one of them came to be" (Ps. 139:13, 16). This is a God who knows you *personally*. Consider God's words to Moses. He says, "I am pleased with you and know you *by name*" (Ex.

33:17). In Isaiah 43:1 God says, "Do not fear, for I have redeemed you; I have summoned you *by name*; you are mine" (emphasis added in the above verses). Twice in Isaiah 45 we see God speaking to His people and claiming He is a God who "summons you by name" (3, 4).

GOD MADE YOU AND KNOWS YOU BY NAME. HE SUMMONS YOU TO BELONG TO HIM.

This God knows you by name. After all, your *name* has been written in the Lamb's book of life as described in the book of Revelation.

God made you and knows you by name. He summons you to belong to Him.

———〰———

When I married my husband, I stood at the altar and pledged my life to a person. I made a covenant vow to a person. I didn't commit to a plan. In fact, without reservation, I committed my life to someone precisely because we didn't know the future. At the altar we essentially cried out, "I'll go anywhere with you! I'll do anything! Who cares? We could be rich, poor, sick, or healthy, and it doesn't matter because we're together!" I'm so glad I understood this because after that marriage ceremony, my husband and I had firm plans that completely fell apart. God ordained a surprise pregnancy, a career change, and medical issues that we simply could not have known about in advance. But we married each other, not a plan. And we loved each other, so that was the basis of our journey together. So powerful is this love drawing lovers together that nothing else matters but their love.

The marriage ceremony reminds me what it means to belong to Jesus in a love relationship, but it's also powerful to think of surrendering to Jesus as a King. When I acknowledge that I belong to Christ and surrender my right to my own life—belonging to a Person and not a plan—every moment of my life invites intimacy with Jesus because He is reigning as my King in those moments. I exist in those moments for Him—to make much of Him and to lay my life down to be used for His purposes—even if I'm unsure of where we are going and what's happening.

Sadly, I spend so much time focusing on knowing my exact plan in life that I lose intimacy with Jesus. I forget about Him in my frantic rushing around to enact my plan. Even my good plans of ministry and service to others can often happen without my abiding deeply with Jesus, the very One for whom I'm chosen. As a picture of what this misplaced focus looks like, I often think about a classic scene in one of the most famous and repeated comedic scenes in film. In an episode of *I Love Lucy*, the beloved sitcom of the 1950s, Lucy is about to have a baby. When this episode premiered on January 19, 1953, more people tuned to watch than the inauguration of Dwight D. Eisenhower[2] the next day. In the episode Ricky, Fred, and Ethel rehearse the perfect plan for when Lucy announces it's time to go to the hospital. Twice the trio calmly and perfectly rehearse their plan: Ricky will help Lucy with her coat, Ethel will call the doctor, and Fred will take the suitcase of Lucy's clothes down to the taxi. It's a foolproof plan.

As soon as Lucy enters the room to tell everyone it's time, total chaos ensues. Instead of calmly caring for Lucy—the most important person and the one all the plans are about—the trio scrambles around, dropping the suitcase of clothes, tripping over one another, and screaming about the taxi. The three rush out the door and leave Lucy behind. She stands there alone in the apartment and says, "Hey! Wait for me!" Finally, when Ricky returns for her, he pushes the door open only to squash Lucy against the wall.

This hilarious scene became a trope in many future movies and sitcoms of the panicky father who forgets his wife in his zeal to enact the plan of going to the hospital. When I think about this scene, I think of how we also have all these perfect plans in place, but we often forget the Person who matters most. We forget Jesus. Everything should have been about Lucy and the new life coming, but instead, the plan got in the way. And when we finally realize we've left Jesus behind, we rush back to Him and wonder where He's hiding, just like Ricky who scolds Lucy and says, "Where are you? This is no time to play games!"[3]

I don't want to forget Jesus. I don't want to push Him behind the door because I misunderstand why I'm chosen. It's for Him. He's what everything is all about—not my frantic plans.

This simple concept of being chosen for Christ helps us focus on the *who* and not the *where, when*, or *how* of our life. Picture yourself being given away to Jesus and saying, "I'll go anywhere with you. I'll do anything. It doesn't matter, as long as we're together."

*W*HO MATTERS AND NOT THE WHERE. IF I'M WITH JESUS, NOTHING ELSE MATTERS. I CAN GO ANYWHERE IF I KNOW THE *WHO*.

Knowing the *who* isn't just about feeling God's love like this; it also comforts us in the most practical ways. For example, in the midst of my travel anxiety, I learned to rest in the *who* and not the *where* or *how*. Having to travel by myself via plane or rental car, on unknown roads in strange cities, nearly demolished my emotional stability. I almost canceled several big events because I didn't want to travel. But then I remembered: *the who matters and not the where.* If I'm with Jesus, nothing else matters. I can be driving alone on a dark road with complete security in God's presence. I can go anywhere if I know the *who.* I'm learning what pastor and theologian A. W. Tozer states so beautifully: "It is wholly impossible for us to know what lies before us, but it is possible to know something vastly more important . . . We cannot know for certain the what and the whither of our earthly pilgrimage, but we can be sure of the Who. And nothing else really matters."[4]

We can be sure of the who.

Nothing else really matters.

Consider the words of Father Jacques Philippe who wrote to aid those seeking more peace in the midst of anxiety:

> The Lord can leave us wanting relative to certain things (sometimes judged indispensable in the eyes of the world), but He never leaves us deprived of what is essential: His presence, His peace, and all that is necessary for the complete fulfillment of our lives, according to His plans for us.[5]

Knowing I have what is "essential" at all times helps me embrace my life as chosen for Christ because what I most need is His presence. Jesus never deprives me of His presence, His peace, and everything I truly need at any moment.

———⟪⟫———

As I move deeper into this chosen life, I am learning to live for a Person—not plans, places, positions, or partnerships. I can tell Jesus that I know I'm chosen for Him. And this means that I can do whatever He asks me to, wherever, and with whomever He brings into my life. Pastor and author Paul David Tripp explains knowing that you exist *for* Christ changes everything, "from the way that you think about your identity, meaning, and purpose to the way that you approach even the most incidental of human duties. Everything that was created was made by God and for God."[6] Learning this, and embracing a lifestyle that lives for Him, has changed everything about how I step into each new day.

I'm chosen for Him, not my plans.

I'm chosen to bring Him glory—to draw attention to His greatness—at all times.

I'm chosen to enjoy His love like a bridegroom has for a bride.

———∞———

"For" works as a vital little word. Embracing our identity as chosen *for* Someone—belonging to Him, existing entirely for His purposes—rips us from a world of self-centeredness. We fix our eyes on Him, not our plans. In Hebrews 12:1–2, I noticed something I had never considered before. It says this:

> Therefore, since we are surrounded by such a great cloud of witnesses, let us throw off everything that hinders and the sin that so easily entangles. And let us run with perseverance the race marked out for us, fixing our eyes on Jesus, the pioneer and perfecter of faith.

For the first time, I considered what this verse *doesn't* say. It doesn't say, "fix your eyes on the race marked out for you." It doesn't say, "look carefully at the course ahead." Instead, it says to fix "our eyes on Jesus." We look at Him most of all, not our plans. That delightful verb "fix" appears in several places in Scripture as an invitation to refocus our heart. I love how David phrases this focus in Psalm 141:8 in the midst of his own confusion. He writes, "But my eyes are fixed on you, Sovereign LORD." Or consider the famous cry in 2 Chronicles 20:12 when King Jehoshaphat feels powerless, afraid, and uncertain. He says to God, "We do not know what to do, but our eyes are on you."

We don't know what to do, but our eyes are on You.

As I talked with several women whose plans fell apart this year—through rejection from people and opportunities—we discussed what it means to live chosen for a Person, not a plan. The truth of the phrase brought comfort and assurance that when life feels out of control, we fix our eyes on the reason for our life: we exist for Jesus.

I want to live chosen, as if I know exactly why I exist. We are chosen for Christ, to make the greatness of Christ more fully known. We are not here to make a name for ourselves, to gain fame, or to attract attention; we're here to make His name great. We can now say, like the prophet Isaiah to the Lord, "Your name and renown are the desire of our hearts" (Isa. 26:8).

I'm no longer waiting for my perfect life to begin. I know that I'm chosen for Christ, and now I'm ready to step into the life I've been missing. I step forward into intimacy with Jesus—knowing who I exist for—because finally, the where, when, and how aren't important. I can look around this ordinary day and proclaim the truth of Romans 11:36: "For from him and through him and for him are all things. To him be the glory forever! Amen."

YOUR NEXT STEP

—⟋⟍—

Read Colossians 1:13–20.

1. What does it mean to you that the point of your existence is "for Christ?"

2. In your own words, write down what it means to you to be chosen for a Person, not a plan.

3. Describe the emotions you might feel when you truly see yourself as a bride of Christ who God summons by name.

4. What do you have to believe about Jesus to go anywhere, at anytime, with whomever He chooses because He's with you?

PART TWO

—⁓⁓—

THE SEVEN
INVITATIONS

—⟋ᴨ⟍—

THE FIRST INVITATION: WORSHIP

"Let my people go, so that they may worship me."
—The Lord speaking
through Moses in Exodus 8:1

I'm pretty sure I'm tone deaf. And I cannot read music. In church during the worship time, I muffle the sound of my voice with my hands or sing into the flowered scarf around my neck. I've even apologized to the family sitting in front of me about my terrible singing voice. My daughters comfort me during the worship time as I grimace over my own warbling, off-key voice. I'm the least musical person I know—vocally, as a dancer, and in creating music on instruments. So when I read about God choosing me to worship Him—and all the worship through song and dance in the Bible—I feel like I'll never be a good worshiper. *Are you sure You chose me to worship You, Jesus? Have You heard this voice?*

Thank goodness worship encompasses vastly more than *singing.*

Worship, I'm learning, is cultivating an awareness of God's presence and responding with joy to Him. Worship, guided by the Holy Spirit, refers to a focus on Jesus and His payment for our sin.

I'm worshiping when I'm praising God and declaring who He is in any situation. Peter tells me I'm chosen for this—to declare His praises—and this chosen reality represents the first invitation to a new way of living.

Every day, I worship. No matter what, I can worship.

When we worship we engage in the most essential, most meaningful, and most authentic thing we can do as human beings. God chose us for this daily experience of worship.

—⟨⟨⟨—

In 2014 Oprah Winfrey, billionaire talk show host and owner of her own television network, published her collection of wisdom gleamed from decades of interviews with the most famous and influential people in the world. Oprah based the book *What I Know for Sure*, on her favorite interview question: "What do you know for sure?"[1]

If Oprah asked me, I know what I would answer after all these years of searching after God. I would say this:

It's always the right decision to worship Jesus. It's never wrong to choose to worship wherever you are. Worshiping Jesus is something you will never regret, and you can never do it too much. When you come to the end of your life, you'll never say, "I wish I spent less time worshiping Jesus." So many times, when I'm not sure what I'm doing, I think, "I can worship here."

A new day begins for you. Think about where you are. Think about the people around you. Think about the tasks and responsibilities in front of you today whether completing work, raising children, attending classes, recovering from illness or injury, keeping a home, or any combination of that list. What if I told you that God chose you to worship Him right now, to experience His presence, to proclaim His greatness, holiness, and perfection? What if the whole point of today with all its challenges and disappointments, and the reason for your life, centers on this one eternal task of worship?

A friend's husband died in a plane crash, leaving her with two young daughters and a new baby. During the funeral we sat down as we sang the hymn "Great is Thy Faithfulness." But then, while we all remained seated, the young widow stood up and lifted her hands into the air to praise God. She praised God—declaring that He was sovereign, good, faithful, and powerful—even at her husband's funeral. I'll never forget the image of her standing up like that and singing with joy while *at the same time* weeping with sorrow. And as she stood up alone in front of us all, the pastor soon walked over to her side, placed his arm around her, and worshiped God with her. She *wasn't alone* in her grief or her worship. We all sang louder, worshiping with her to announce God's faithfulness even in death. Days later, the young woman told me of the comfort and intimacy she felt with Jesus that enabled her to worship Him and acknowledge His authority in her life. She worshiped—knowing God's presence and declaring His power—during the worst season of her life.

Living with an increasing awareness of God's presence and announcing more and more His character represents the most special and significant invitation to a new way of living. It's an invitation to live as worshipers every day of our lives *no matter what's happening around us.* Think of David's beautiful cry in Psalm 34:1: "I will extol the LORD at all times; his praise will always be on my lips."

At all times. Always.

God chooses people to worship Him at all times, always. A. W. Tozer, who believed "worship is the Christian's full-time occupation," explains our purpose in Christ like this:

[Worship] is why man was created; that is man's chief end.

Apart from that, we have no more idea why we are here. God gave you a harp and placed it in your own heart. God made you in order that you might stand up and charm the rest of the universe as you sing praises to the Lord Jesus Christ.[2]

Picture us standing up to "charm the rest of the universe." When looking at Tozer's life, others would say, "His one daily exercise was the practice of the presence of God, pursuing Him with all his time and energy. To him, Jesus Christ was a daily wonder, a recurring astonishment, a continual amazement of love and grace."[3] What if our daily exercise involved living a life of daily wonder and continual amazement? What if we lived with a joyful expectation of God's fresh presence in our lives each new morning as we worshiped Him?

The story of the Bible essentially defines the single verb, worship. Do you remember *why* the Lord set His people free from slavery in Egypt? He instructs Moses to tell Pharaoh, "Let my people go, so that they may worship me" (Ex. 9:1, 13). In fact, you'll see that word "worship" numerous times in the Old Testament, and you can read God's specifications for where and how He wanted to be worshiped in both Exodus and Leviticus. If you read these books of the Bible, you would see the importance of the *place* of worship (in a tabernacle or temple) and the *procedure* of worship (through a blood sacrifice of an animal via a priest). You may, like most people, have many questions about why we no longer worship God like this.

What makes the coming of Jesus Christ so revolutionary and so astonishing is that He is a Savior who forever transforms the place and procedure of our worship. Now, we worship differently—not in a special place like a tabernacle but in " Spirit and in truth" (John 4:24)—because the temple of God forms now within our very hearts. When we receive Christ, we are now "God's temple" (1 Cor. 3:16–17). Paul reminds believers again in 1 Corinthians 6:19 that we worship in a different, internal temple when he questions, "Do you not know that your bodies are temples of the Holy Spirit, who is in you, whom you have received from God?" Worshiping God from this temple within us means that *wherever we go*, we receive the invitation to worship.

Where are you right now? What's happening? Now think about this: God invites you to worship Him *here*.

But what is worship? How are we to do it? If we're not in a temple and sacrificing animals, what procedure do we follow?

Do not worry if you feel overwhelmed or confused about worship. If you chose to surrender to Jesus and give up your right to yourself, you've actually begun the most significant part of worship: offering yourself as a "living sacrifice." In Romans 12:1 Paul calls this offering of yourself your "true and proper worship." Worship involves this offering of yourself first of all. In the morning you might say, "Jesus, I offer myself to You as a living sacrifice. I surrender every part of this day to You. I serve at Your pleasure today." And that's just the very beginning of the beautiful life we miss when we misunderstand our identity as chosen worshipers.

The Holy Spirit within you teaches you how to worship. According to Philippians 3:3, we "worship by the Spirit of God" (ESV). As I studied theologians and read the Scriptures concerning worship, I began to understand that everything about our worship centers on Jesus Christ, His blood sacrifice for us, and the empowering of the Holy Spirit to enable worship. Tozer explains, "It is impossible to worship God acceptably apart from the Holy Spirit.

The operation of the Spirit of God within us enables us to worship God acceptably through that person we call Jesus Christ, who is Himself God. Therefore, worship originates with God, comes back to us and is reflected from us. That is the worship God accepts, and He accepts no other kind."[4]

When I think about the kind of worship God accepts, it has everything to do with Jesus Christ; I know that my focus on Jesus—knowing I'm chosen for Christ—isn't misplaced or somehow uninformed. And I also know that no other religion offers this acceptable form of worship to God.

I remember the day I read and understood Philippians 2:9–11 and what it means to bring glory to God by worshiping Jesus Christ. Paul writes about Jesus that, "God exalted him to the highest place and gave him the name that is above every name, that at the name of Jesus every knee should bow, in heaven and on earth and under the earth, and every tongue acknowledge that Jesus Christ is Lord, to the glory of God the Father." It brings glory to God the Father when we worship Jesus as Lord and bow before Him. This focus on Jesus delights God the Father. The disciples in John 6:28–29 asked, like I so often do, "What must we do to do the works God requires?" Jesus answered, "The work of God is this: to believe in the one he has sent." As I declare that Jesus is Lord and repeat the gospel to myself each new morning, I am worshiping in the way that most pleases God the Father.

But then what? Maybe, like me, you move into a day of childcare, chores, and career tasks. Where does our worship go now? Theologian Wayne Grudem writes, "Everything in our life should be an act of worship. . . . worship is something we do especially when we come into God's presence, when we are conscious of adoration of him in our hearts, and when we praise him with our voice and speak about him so others may hear. . . . Worship is therefore a direct expression of our ultimate purpose for living."[5] Grudem, like other theologians, uses words indicating that worship, essentially, refers to an awareness of God's presence and a conscious adoration of Him. This sharper vision of God isn't something reserved for our church services or even when we are singing a song to God; it's recognizing who God is in every situation of our lives.

Recognizing God in every situation? Can you imagine?

I think about cleaning toilets (this must happen every week), passing a kidney stone (this happened), and cleaning dog poop off my shoe (yes, this happened).

Is God really here and active? We're told in Psalm 105:4 to "seek his face always," and in Psalm 139 we learn we cannot escape the presence of the Lord even if we tried. This "presence of God" brings refreshment to our souls (Acts 3:19) and is always available to us by the Holy Spirit. As I think about the presence of God, I realize that as I grow in my faith, Jesus leads me to plans, people, and places that help me cultivate a deeper awareness of Him.

I'm *here* because it helps me see Him.

SOMETHING ABOUT WHAT'S HAPPENING TO YOU RIGHT NOW HELPS YOU EXPERIENCE GOD'S PRESENCE MORE.

You're *there*—wherever there is—because it helps you see Him. Something about what's happening to you right now helps you experience God's presence more.

Everything I'm experiencing helps me worship. What I do changes moment by moment, but God stays the same. I can worship Him for His power, beauty, and goodness whether I'm in the grocery store, at church, or even in the shower. I can worship Him in trouble or in ease. Worship leader Matt Redman reminds his audiences, "We can always find a reason to praise. Situations change for better or for worse, but God's worth never changes."[6]

I know I'm worshiping God when I feel more aware of His presence and His unchanging goodness in every situation. I'm chosen by God to experience Him in an intimate, loving way. Grudem tells us, "When we worship God he meets with us and directly ministers to us, strengthening our faith, intensifying our awareness of his presence, and granting refreshment to our spirits."[7] Grudem highlights that we worship God in the midst of needing care; we come to Him for strength because we feel weak; we come to Him for refreshment because we feel weary; we come to Him because we need Him. We need to meet with God. We don't need Jesus to necessarily change anything because we *just need Him*. It's like what Elisabeth Elliot famously said: "The secret is Christ in me, not me in a different set of circumstances."[8]

In any situation—whether suffering disappointment, battling illness, moving through mundane tasks, or in physical danger—chosen people ask, "How can I worship God in this moment? If I truly believe I'm chosen to worship Jesus in this situation, can I declare His praises right now?" For years I wrestled with the command in 1 Thessalonians 5:18 to give thanks in all circumstances "for this is God's will for you in Christ Jesus," and lately I've realized more and more the invitation to worship God for His power, goodness, sufficiency, mercy, beauty, and love—no matter what the situation. We worship God in even the most difficult circumstances.

This past year I grew most of all as a worshiper. I'd been traveling around the country—in a regular old cardigan and loafers and thermos of coffee— speaking on the astonishing concept that God chose us to worship Him in every circumstance of our lives. I could speak with confidence because I had studied the Scriptures concerning worship and these truths trained my eyes to see *divine activity* wherever I go based on His character including His providential care, His provision of all we need, and His eternal perspective. You can remember how to look for divine activity in your own life with these three words: providence, provision, and perspective.

Providence—God arranges all the circumstances of your life in advance for your good and His glory. Providence refers to the protective care of God at all times and the ordering of events to care for our future. He has the power "to bring everything under his control" (Phil. 3:21) and is always working on our behalf. *Because we trust in God's providential care, we can worship Him in any situation. Nothing happens by accident.*

When I think of God ordering events to care for me, I think of a lifetime of stories where I found myself in the right place at the right time to experience God's care even when I was scared or in pain. Recently, our daughter underwent testing for a medical condition that terrified me. At the same time, our ministry assignment would place us in Colorado for the entire summer. How would God care for my daughter when we would leave our network of providers in Pennsylvania? What if something happened to her? How could I worship Him when, clearly, He was sending us away right when my daughter needed help?

As I chose to remember God's providence to arrange events to care for us, I received a phone call from a fellow missionary who knew we needed medical care in Colorado. She told me the name of a doctor in Denver who not only took our insurance but who also had available appointments and happened to be one of the world's leading specialists in the area of our concern. This doctor far surpassed any medical care we would have received in Pennsylvania.

I felt out of control while God never let anything about our daughter fall outside His providential care.

Provision—It is God's nature to ceaselessly provide for His chosen ones. He never stops providing; He cannot help but remain true to His nature as provider. In Genesis 22:14 we see the name of God is Jehovah-Jirah—the LORD Who Provides. This name of God tells us that God sees to it that our *every need* is met.

When I feel discouraged about my day, I often imagine Jesus asking me, "What do you need? How can I provide for you today?" I recite to my heart Psalm 46:1 and remember that the Lord is an "ever-present help in trouble" and that He is a God who will "meet all [our] needs according to the riches of his glory in Christ Jesus" (Phil. 4:19).

I remember the great promise of Hebrews 4:16 and the confidence we have to approach God for help in our time of need. I often think of physical provision—money, shelter, transportation, medical care, or any variety of needs—when I think of how God will provide, but lately I remember the promise that God gives me a boundless supply of His presence (that He gives without limit) and His love (that He pours into our hearts). *Because of God's provision, I can open my eyes to see how He is providing and worship Him in any situation I'm in.* Just as God providentially arranged circumstances for our trip to Colorado, He fully intended to provide in that very place.

Perspective—God offers us an "eternal perspective" on our situation, no matter how difficult. An eternal perspective means we can fix our eyes on eternal, not temporal, things. In 2 Corinthians 4:18 we see the advice to look at eternal things and not temporary worldly things.

But what is eternal? Only three things will last forever: God Himself, God's Word (Matt. 24:35), and the eternal souls of people. When I look at my day, I ask myself how this situation invites me to see God, to

ONLY THREE THINGS WILL LAST FOREVER: GOD HIMSELF, GOD'S WORD, AND THE ETERNAL SOULS OF PEOPLE.

draw upon strength from His Word, and to connect with people He created who do not know Him. Because God offers me an eternal perspective, I can rise above my circumstances to look at what God is doing for kingdom purposes here. As our family sat in the hospital in Denver, we began to talk to the doctor about how God used him to answer our prayer, calm our fears, and provide. We talked about God's providential care. As I spoke about Jesus in that place, I wondered if my daughter's physical needs had something to do with talking to this doctor about Jesus.

—⁓—

Could it be that we're in our discouraging situation so God will draw us to depend on Him, to treasure His Word, and to position us to connect with someone who needs to know Him? Is this situation I'm in an invitation to worship?

At the University of Michigan I memorized a presentation of the gospel because I wanted God to use me in the lives of people. I couldn't imagine anything more exciting than leading someone to know Jesus. Evangelism helped me worship God and kept me holding on to an eternal perspective even in the midst of a grueling class and teaching schedule. At that time, however, I battled so much stress and anxiety that I would grind my teeth all through the night. To save my jaw and teeth, the dentist suggested an expensive, custom-designed mouthguard that would cost a small fortune—something I definitely didn't have as a graduate student. That Sunday in church, I asked a couple I hardly knew to pray for me about that mouthguard. I needed God to provide; I felt so helpless and dependent on Him. But I wanted to worship Jesus right in the midst of my need.

The man praying for me looked up and said, "I'm a dentist. Come to my office, and I will make your mouthguard for free." I couldn't believe God's providential ordering of events to place me next to a couple who happened to have a dental practice, to prompt me to pray with them, and to invite them to respond to me. I couldn't believe God's provision, and I rejoiced in my heart over what a great God I served who could meet such a specific need so immediately. That next week I arrived at the dentist's office, and as his hygienist prepared my mouth, she casually asked how I heard about their dental practice.

With a mouthful of equipment, I slurred, "I prayed at church, and God answered me!"

The woman looked down at my face, and she said, "You pray? You pray to God? And He answers you?" Her eyes welled up in tears. She sat back, took off her gloves, and wiped her eyes.

I wondered if my month of stress and teeth grinding were ordained by God; my heart jumped at the recognition of a divine moment. I worshiped Jesus for offering me this eternal perspective even as I sat with a mouth still dripping with molding clay for my mouthguard. I jammed my hand into my purse that sat beside me to find the booklet explaining the gospel that I kept there just in case God gave me an opportunity just like this.

"Yes!" I warbled. "I do pray. And God does answer me. And He will answer you. Has anyone ever shared with you how you can know Jesus personally?" This was my first time using my new evangelism tool, a little booklet about knowing God personally. I handed the gospel presentation to her. "Read this," I said, finally able to rinse my mouth. I quickly summarized the gospel—how God loved us and created us to know Him personally, how our sin separated us from a holy God, how Jesus came to provide the payment for our sin, and how we can individually receive the free gift of salvation.

As I left, I gave her my phone number. That evening she called my home and said, "I prayed that prayer at the back of the booklet. Now what do I do?"

"Come to church with me!" I said, so full of joy I could hardly keep from jumping up and down in my apartment. Suddenly, the stress of my life didn't matter. The jaw grinding wasn't important. What mattered is that God arranged a situation in my life to proclaim the gospel. My heart exploded in worship that night.

———

I want to conclude with *the most important part of worship*. The most important part of worship—and what energizes, reinforces, and purifies worship—is the understanding that a holy God sent His Son to die for our sins. If you read the accounts of worship in Isaiah 6 and Revelation 15, we worship God *because of His holiness*. In Revelation 5, we worship God *because He is worthy of our worship*. We read, "Worthy is the Lamb, who was slain . . ." We worship Him as the Lamb of God who takes away sins. Whether or not He ever shows us His providential care, provision, or invites us into eternal moments of evangelism, we still worship Him because of who He is.

I'm going to say that again: we still worship Him *because of who He is.*

Think about Peter, the one who declares to us our chosen identity as worshipers, and his response to God's miraculous provision of fish in Luke 5:1–11. If you remember the story, Jesus asks Peter to put his nets down for a catch even though he "worked hard all night" and didn't catch one fish (v. 5). When Peter obeys Jesus, he catches so many fish that the nets begin to break. What I love about this passage is that Peter doesn't focus on the miraculous catch of fish. In fact, he falls at Jesus' feet and says, "Go away from me, Lord; I am a sinful man!" (v. 8). Peter doesn't focus on the provision. He looks at His Savior who has far more power than catching fish. This is a Holy God who offers forgiveness of sin. Peter and the fishermen leave everything to follow Jesus into a new ministry of "catching men."

They are worshipers; they looked at Jesus and didn't rest in the enjoyment of a miracle.

Sadly, when I think about being chosen to worship, I want the miracle and not the Miracle Worker. Do you remember *Charlotte's Web* by E. B. White? In the story a spider named Charlotte attempts to save a pig's life by declaring some beautiful things about him in her web. The pig Wilbur becomes famous as Charlotte writes "Some Pig," "Terrific," "Radiant," and "Humble." What's fascinating about this book is how a spider can write, yet the focus is on the pig.

A *spider* can write.

A spider can *write*, and a pig gets all the attention. We focus on the miracle not the Miracle Worker. When the farmer, Mr. Zuckerman, sees the amazing words written in the web, he tells his wife that surely they have "no ordinary pig." Mrs. Zuckerman says it best when she responds, "It seems to me you're a little off. It seems to me we have no ordinary spider."[9]

I love this moment in *Charlotte's Web* because it teaches me how quickly I look at God's blessing instead of God Himself. Wilbur becomes more and more famous even though Charlotte is the real marvel. In the same way, I think of Luke 5 as a promise that if I just trust Jesus, He will fill my nets with success. Jesus will save whatever it is I want to save and promote—just like Charlotte saving and promoting Wilbur the pig.

It turns out that the greatest catch in Luke 5 isn't the fish; it's that Peter catches on to who Jesus actually is.

It turns out that the greatest catch in Luke 5 isn't the fish; it's that Peter catches on to who Jesus actually is.

Knowing Jesus and worshiping Him is always a greater joy than any physical blessing He might provide.

The miraculous catch of fish shows us a miracle of provision—that we see throughout Scripture in God's provision of clothing in the garden of Eden, of a substitute for Isaac on the altar, of manna in the wilderness, of never-ending oil for the widow through Elisha—but what's so beautiful and so powerful is that this miracle, like all the others, pales in comparison to knowing the Miracle Worker.

We see this idea that Jesus is greater than any success in the cry of David in Psalm 63:3 who says about God, "Because your love is better than life, my lips will glorify you," and in the song of the priest in Psalm 84:10 who writes, "Better is one day in your courts than a thousand elsewhere." Throughout the Bible we see how knowing God is better than anything we could ever desire.

When I finished reading the story in Luke 5, I found myself praying what David prays in Psalm 51:12: "Restore to me the joy of your salvation." Peter saw his sin. He didn't care about fish. Peter saw a Savior, and nothing else mattered. The greatest need of our hearts is forgiveness before a Holy God who then invites us to *worship Him.*

YOUR NEXT STEP

Read Revelation 5:11–14.

1. How would you describe worship to someone? How do you worship God?

2. Describe a time when you were able to worship God because of His providence, provision, or the eternal perspective He provided?

3. Do you think it's possible to worship as a "full-time occupation"? What did Tozer mean by this?

4. Explain what Elisabeth Elliot means when she says, "The secret is Christ in me, not me in a different set of circumstances."

———ᴧᴧ———

THE SECOND INVITATION: LIVE AS GOD'S TREASURED POSSESSION

"For you are a people holy to the LORD your God. Out of all the peoples on the face of the earth, the LORD has chosen you to be his treasured possession."

—DEUTERONOMY 14:2

God never withholds from His child that which His love and wisdom call good. God's refusals are always merciful —"severe mercies" at times but mercies all the same. God never denies us our heart's desire except to give us something better.

—MISSIONARY ELISABETH ELLIOT

Your chosen life isn't about worship only. If it were, that would be enough to fill the rest of our days with joy in adoring Jesus. But God offers another invitation to a chosen life that changes everything about how you live your day. In Psalm 65:4 David writes, "Blessed are those you choose and bring near to live in your courts! We are filled with the good things of your house, of your holy temple."

Chosen people enjoy the "good things" of the Lord all day

long. Do you know why we can? Because God chose us as His treasured possession to display His lavish love and goodness to us. I became a different woman when I saw myself as *God's treasured possession*. I woke up with the expectation that God would attend to me as someone He greatly values and cares for.

Moses reveals to us in Deuteronomy 7:6 (similarly repeated in 14:2 and 26:18): "For you are a people holy to the LORD your God. The LORD your God has chosen you out of all the peoples on the face of the earth to be his people, his treasured possession."

Throughout the Bible we learn that we are God's treasured possession. This promise refers not only to the Israelites, but as we see in the book of Ephesians, to every believer today. We learn in Ephesians 1 that Gentiles—all non-Jews then and today—are also included in Christ and are "God's possession" (vv. 13–14). In fact, the whole point of Ephesians aims to convince the Gentiles that they are "fellow citizens with God's people" (2:19), "sharers together" in God's promise through Jesus (3:6), and equally receiving the "boundless riches of Christ" (3:8). We live today with the assurance that the promise of living as God's treasured possession did not apply only to a certain group of people in a certain time in history.

We are His treasured possession now.

How had I missed this? How could I have lived for four decades and not seen myself as the treasured, special possession of God who treats me with tender, careful, extravagant love? That phrase "treasured possession" reminds me of a rare jewel. God even describes us this way in Isaiah 62:3, that God's people are "a crown of splendor in the LORD's hand, a royal diadem in the hand of [our] God."

If you know anything about the royal Crown Jewels of the United Kingdom, you probably picture St. Edward's Crown, used to coronate all the British monarchs since the thirteenth century. This special crown rests in the Jewel House at the Tower of London. The Crown Jewels—comprising 140 royal, precious, and treasured ceremonial objects—rest under constant surveillance by over a hundred hidden cameras and the Tower Guard of twenty-two personnel.[1] The treasured objects also stay under the protection of bombproof glass.[2]

Consider the protection. Consider the value. Consider the beauty of this display.

You are a treasured possession, a rare jewel in the Lord's hand.

The closest I have come to this kind of value and beauty in rare jewels is the Splendor of Diamonds exhibit at the Smithsonian Museum of Natural History where you can view the seven rarest and most valuable diamonds in the world—sometimes worth hundreds of millions of dollars. If I owned something like this, I would take *such good care of it*. I would never let it out of my sight. I would brag about it and invite everyone I knew to see it, too.

I wonder, though, if the Tower Guard or the Smithsonian security personnel would *die* to protect the jewels. Would they give their *lives* for them? If you're wondering about living as God's treasured possession, your first realization is that God sent His Son to die for us. This declaration of God's goodness fills our hearts to overflowing without any other example of God's love for us. We are that precious, that valuable to Him.

Several times in the Old Testament we see God's declaration that we are His *treasured possession*; in the New Testament we see in Titus 2:14 that God chooses us to redeem and purify us through Christ to become a people that are Christ's "very own" (NIV) or his

THE QUESTION STANDS, THEN: HOW DOES GOD TREAT US AS HIS TREASURED POSSESSION? "own possession" (ESV). We also see the description of our identity in Christ in Ephesians 1:14 as "God's possession" and as His "special possession" in 1 Peter 2:9.

The question stands, then: How does God treat us as His treasured possession?

Believing in the overwhelming and incomprehensible goodness of God at all times on my behalf represents one of the most fulfilling challenges of my whole life—perhaps it's a challenge for you too. What would it mean, for example, to believe it—to truly, deeply, really believe it—when God says in Jeremiah 32:40 about how God treats His people: "I will never stop doing good to them"? Or in Romans 10:12 when Paul proclaims, "There is no difference between Jew and Gentile—the same Lord is Lord of all and richly blesses all who call on him"? This is a God who "richly provides us with everything for our enjoyment" (1 Tim. 6:17). This is a God who "satisfies your desires with good things so that your youth is renewed like the eagle's" (Ps. 103:5). This is a God who "delights in the well-being" of His people (Ps. 35:27).

And we already have Jesus! We already have the greatest gift we can imagine in Jesus providing payment for our sin, yet God still does more. As we saw in the references above,

He never stops doing good to you.
He richly blesses you.
He richly provides everything for your enjoyment.
He satisfies your desires with good things.
He delights in your well-being.

As His treasured possession in Christ, He is abounding in love toward us who call on Him (Ps. 86:5). He releases His goodness stored up for us (Ps. 31:19). And each new day of our lives, we can wake up to the new, good compassions of God (Lam. 3:23).

God chose us to live as His treasured possession. I have been teaching my daughters this truth all year long, and sometimes God makes us laugh and tear up with joy when we see evidence that we are so treasured by Him.

In light of our desire to understand fully our identity as God's treasured possession—and to identify His lavish care for us—I reminded my daughters one morning to look for evidence of God's special care for them. We were driving to church, and my youngest daughter cried out, "Well, to tell you the truth, I'm really craving chocolate right now. I wish I had a piece of chocolate! I'm serious. All I can think about is chocolate."

It was a strange craving and a silly conversation. As I go back to my lesson on living like God's treasured possession, Kate keeps interrupting me about her desire for chocolate.

At that moment, I opened up the compartment next to my steering wheel to get a tissue, and a lovely piece of Ghirardelli chocolate, wrapped in blue foil, sat there as if delivered from heaven. "How did this get here?" I said and laughed. "Kate! It's for you. God seems to have sent this. See, I told you you are His treasured possession!" I reached behind me to hand her the chocolate.

As she ate the chocolate, we laughed about the bizarre and over-the-top chocolate craving and God's timing to provide some for her. I tilted my head to the side as I turned into the church parking lot. I wondered about that chocolate. Did God really provide it? Had He really heard Kate?

We walked in to church, still delighted, and still wondering about God's answer to Kate's desire for chocolate. And then we saw it: in the café of our church, the staff designed a prayer station with the words, "Taste and see that the Lord is good!" with a silver platter on which a pile of chocolate rose high as an invitation for each person to enjoy a piece.

Each person would enjoy *chocolate* as a sign of God's goodness. As a man held out the platter of chocolate to Kate, my jaw dropped. I blurted out, "You've got to be kidding, God!"

Kate's eyes sparkled as she took *another piece of chocolate*. She looked up at me in disbelief, and I thought about this memory imprinting itself onto her soul as one of a thousand other demonstrations of God's love over her lifetime. But on this day it was a platter of chocolate and a blue Ghirardelli. On this day God showed His lavish love, and we still talk about Kate's Day of Chocolate.

God didn't neglect our older daughter, either. Around that same time Sarah was crying one night because she felt lonely and separated from her friends while we traveled to a ministry conference. She was miserable in the hotel room and certain that she'd never feel better again, especially because her New Year's Eve plans had fallen through. I stood in the hotel room with her, and I said, "God has not made a mistake. We're here because He chose for us to be here. And you are His chosen, treasured possession. Let's ask God to remind you how dearly loved you are and how special you are to Him. Sarah, you are His treasured possession!"

At that exact moment Sarah's phone began to buzz with texts from friends who were just "randomly" thinking of her. And as we went to the lobby to find some dinner, we found that the restaurant featured her absolute favorite meal of all time: shrimp and grits. I was in awe because I knew how rare it was to find a restaurant serving such an item (unless you're in Louisiana!). We smiled at each other because we both read this reality through the filter of God's love for her.

We collect evidence and store it in our hearts. We love this God who one day provided chocolate and shrimp and grits for girls who needed to know the lavish love of God. We were looking for evidence, and God provided it.

—⁂—

This morning I read in Matthew 7:11 Jesus' words about good gifts. He says, "If you, then, though you are evil, know how to give good gifts to your children, how much more will your Father in heaven give good things to those who ask him!" Our heavenly Father gives good things to us; in fact, we read this same statement in Luke 11:13 of the good gift of the Holy Spirit. We also read that this gift—perhaps the greatest gift in the world—arrives to us "without limit" (John 3:34).

What if we believed this? What if we woke up with expectation that God would deliver good things into our hands? What if you collected evidence even today of this goodness? What if our fellowship with other Christians involved our stories of how God bestowed His goodness? I would love to sit across the table from you and hear all about His goodness to you. I would want you to lean in and say what the psalmist says in Psalm 66:16: "Come and hear . . . let me tell you what he has done for me."

And I wonder, too, if your evidence of God's love for you came even through hardship. I wonder if, like me, you can rejoice in what God has done through pain and suffering. I would sip coffee with you and say the words of Psalm 119:71 as I talk about depression and anxiety. I would say this: "It was good for me to be afflicted so that I might learn your decrees."

We live as His treasured possession. Even when we go through murky times when we cannot perceive God's work on our behalf, we step forward into the faith that God sees us, hears us, and is at work. When I don't see any physical evidence of being treasured, I remember that the best thing that could ever happen to me is being *with Jesus*. He treasures me with His comforting presence while I wait for whatever blessing He has in store. One day God's deliverance will come, and we'll proclaim what the psalmist writes in Psalm 40:1–5:

> I waited patiently for the LORD;
>   he turned to me and heard my cry.
> He lifted me out of the slimy pit,
>   out of the mud and mire;
> he set my feet on a rock
>   and gave me a firm place to stand.
> He put a new song in my mouth,
>   a hymn of praise to our God.
> Many will see and fear the LORD
>   and put their trust in him.
>
> Blessed is the one
>   who trusts in the LORD,
> who does not look to the proud,
>   to those who turn aside to false gods.
> Many, LORD my God,
>   are the wonders you have done,
>   the things you planned for us.
> None can compare with you;

were I to speak and tell of your deeds,
they would be too many to declare.

As God's treasured possession, we wait patiently and know God hears us. He will lift us out of the mud, set us down in a firm place, and give us reasons to praise Him. We look forward to the wonderful things planned for us that will be "too many to declare." I pray we see ourselves as the treasured possession of God, chosen for Christ, and that God would reveal to us how treasured we are if we would look and see. He "daily bears our burdens" (Ps. 68:19); we can tell Him every-

AS GOD'S TREASURED POSSESSION, WE WAIT PATIENTLY AND KNOW GOD HEARS US. HE WILL LIFT US OUT OF THE MUD, SET US DOWN IN A FIRM PLACE, AND GIVE US REASONS TO PRAISE HIM.

thing we need and "wait expectantly" for His provision (Ps. 5:3). It's thrilling to think that God will show you His special, attentive care, even right now.

In Psalm 23—perhaps the most memorized and treasured of all the psalms for many people—we read about God as our Good Shepherd. Recently I spent time meditating on the first three verses of this psalm, and the insight from the Holy Spirit about the "verbs of God" helped me understand myself in light of how God treats me as His treasured possession. We read this in the stately language of the English Standard Version:

The LORD is my shepherd; I shall not want.
   He makes me lie down in green pastures.
He leads me beside still waters.
   He restores my soul.
He leads me in paths of righteousness
   for his name's sake.

With God as our Shepherd, we shall never want or lack for anything. We will always have exactly what we need. But then, look at what God does. He "makes" us lie down—even when we don't want to or perceive we need to. He arranges our circumstances for rest; he orchestrates the scenario in which we *must rest*.

During one particularly painful event in my life, I understood God as a Good Shepherd. I had exhausted myself with an overbooked travel and speaking schedule in the midst of writing, teaching two classes, serving on a committee, keeping the house, and raising our two teen daughters. As I talked to God about not feeling like His treasured possession in the midst of the exhaustion, feelings of dread, and a daily sense of being overwhelmed, I suddenly endured a kidney stone that kept me bedridden for days. It *completely immobilized* me. Having canceled a speaking engagement in San Antonio, I collapsed onto my bed, thinking about how God had "made me lie down" to rest. While I wouldn't wish a kidney stone on anyone, I did find myself worshiping Jesus for His sovereignty and divine activity during that week to *make me lie down*. During that time of silence and rest, I connected more deeply with Jesus, my family, and my sweet neighbors who brought meals and encouraging conversations. I rejoiced in Jesus as my Good Shepherd. I felt strangely refreshed and restored.

As I thought about this Good Shepherd who makes us lie down

to rest, I also considered with joy the notion of "green pastures" and "still waters." I have a hard time picturing myself in these places during the bitter cold of a Pennsylvania winter, so I began to wonder about the places God leads us that He designs to restore our soul and bring glory to Him.

HOW FREEING AND RELAXING TO THINK ABOUT GOD PLANNING OUR *PERFECT PLACES OF REST* AND ACTIVELY LEADING US TO THOSE PLACES.

We cannot imagine these places, but He can.

We do not design these places, but He does.

How freeing and relaxing to think about God planning our *perfect places of rest* and actively leading us to those places. He is a God who leads us to "undisturbed places of rest" (Isa. 32:18) and, more importantly, creates the conditions in which we go to Jesus as our perfect rest.

Chosen men and women know they live as God's treasured possession, even when life looks hard or uncomfortable. They know that He invites us to rest by green pastures and still waters because, in every situation, we have *exactly what we need*. Sometimes, however, God strips away our physical comforts to help us see Him as our true rest.

I recently memorized Psalm 62:1–2: "Truly my soul finds rest in God; my salvation comes from him. Truly he is my rock and my salvation; he is my fortress, I will never be shaken." The original language implies "He alone." In Him *only* do we find our rest and our salvation. David repeats the concept in verse 5: "Yes, my soul, find rest in God; my hope comes from him," that is, from Him only. He continues in verse 6: "Truly he [only God] is my rock and my salvation; he is my fortress, I will not be shaken."

My soul finds rest in God only. Only Him.

I traveled to a resort in Colorado so thrilled to teach the women all about resting in God alone. Of course, what drew me to this speaking event included the promise of floating in the mountain hot springs under the golden aspen trees, stargazing at night, and hiking to cool pools high in the Rocky Mountains. I couldn't wait! I knew God would lead me to the still waters and all those wide open spaces I needed to restore my soul. I packed my bathing suit, my hiking gear, and all my hopes and dreams for a four-day spa retreat and flew across the country to the mountains.

And within a few hours of arriving I felt the harsh reality of altitude sickness that kept me in my cabin *for the entire four days*. I emerged only to give my presentations to the women who returned from the hot springs, stargazing, and hiking. As I returned to my cabin, I chuckled with Jesus about how He was truly teaching me that my soul finds rest in *God alone*. I didn't need anything else. I had peace in my heart and the joy of the Lord like never before. And I didn't miss a thing because I was with the One my heart desires.

YOUR NEXT STEP

Read Psalm 23.

1. How would you live differently if you experienced yourself as Christ's treasured possession?

2. How does God treasure you?

3. Write down some examples of when you felt like a treasured jewel in God's hand. How did He display His lavish care and attention to you?

4. What in your life tempts you to feel less than God's treasured possession?

CHAPTER 7

THE THIRD INVITATION:
BELONG TO
A NEW FAMILY

God sets the lonely in families...
—PSALM 68:6

*You are no longer foreigners and strangers, but fellow citizens with
God's people and also members of his household.*
—EPHESIANS 2:19

After I married my husband, Ashley—a man from a small
southern town called Fuquay-Varina, North Carolina—his
sister-in-law, Lori, handed me a large piece of paper that she un-
rolled like a scroll. "This will help you know who everyone is," she
said. I looked down at a family tree that included all my husband's
grandparents, great aunts and great uncles, aunts, uncles, cousins,
second cousins, and on and on—on both sides. I had married into
an enormous southern family so rooted to North Carolina that
some of the street names represented my new "kinfolk."

At one of the first wedding parties I attended with Ashley,
a woman approached me and asked in a southern accent where

all the words came out long and wispy, like taffy: "Now, who are your people?" We all long to know "our people."

I remember the first time I read and understood Psalm 68:6 and how God "sets the lonely in families" as a graduate student in Michigan. I joined a small Presbyterian church. Hungry for God and with a profound need to belong somewhere, I attached to this church and not only faithfully attended Sunday school and church, but I also volunteered in the youth group and joined the weekly prayer team. I even attended congregational meetings. I would look around me at all those people as my new aunts and uncles and my new brothers and sisters. Tears formed in my eyes because I felt so connected to these Presbyterians who took in a lonely graduate student who wanted so much to know Jesus and walk with Him.

When we become Christians, we join the family of God or what Paul calls "God's household" (Eph. 2:19). In this family you take on a special role. At all times you receive the unlimited privileges of belonging as a child in a royal household, and you also accept the invitation to bless others within this family. In other words, you're a child (dependent), but you're also a sister or brother (encourager) and a mother or father (shepherd). As you grow in your Christian faith you'll find God using you more and more—with the special gifts He has given you—to help others mature in their faith "until we all reach unity in the faith and in the knowledge of the Son of God and become mature, attaining to the whole measure of the fullness of Christ" (Eph. 4:13).

As if worshiping Jesus and living as His treasured possession weren't enough to fill our days with joy, we are also chosen for Christ to belong to a new family. And in this family we belong. The desire in your heart to know your "people"—to feel connected and secure and rooted—dissolves into your new chosen identity as *belonging to a new family.* In this family we not only mature, but we also help others mature. If you live confused about your calling in the Lord, you can rest assured that you know at least one reason God chose you: to enjoy belonging to and serving within His family.

—⁓—

In Galatians 6:10, we read how we belong to the "family of believers." This family spreads far and wide, not just what we think of when we think of the local church. Paul talks about God's family "throughout" the land (1 Thess. 4:10), and Peter describes this family united "throughout the world" (1 Peter 5:9). Remarkably, in this family of God, Jesus calls us His "brothers and sisters" (Heb. 2:11). When Jesus chose you for Himself, He did so to place you in His household.

I love knowing I'm part of a *new family*. Maybe your family background isn't necessarily godly, healthy, or hopeful. You might feel doomed to repeat certain patterns of addiction, mental instability, or any kind of brokenness. You might feel like you can never break free from your DNA. No matter how hard you try, you're going to end up in a predetermined way, with certain mannerisms and inclinations to sin. And maybe you're reading this, and the notion of family—even that very word—stings your heart. It's a bitter word because perhaps you were abandoned; perhaps you have no mother or father, no wise older sister or protective brother, no playful and admiring little siblings. Perhaps you've never felt the encircling love of grandparents and aunts and uncles and cousins that provide a security and sense of identity in your life. Maybe you have spent most of your life learning to forgive your family.

I bring great news to your heart: when you received Christ, you became a "new creation" (2 Cor. 5:17), and God brought you into

His glorious household (Eph. 2:19). God clearly has redeemed you "from the empty way of life handed down to you from your ancestors" (1 Peter 1:18). If you described the "empty way of life" you wish you could rise above, remember His redeeming love to make you a new person, in a new family, with new patterns to follow.

God also cares so much about you feeling part of the family —especially when you've lost your physical family—that He commands us many times in Scripture to care for orphans, widows, and the fatherless. James 1:27 explains how God accepts our religion as "pure and faultless" if we "look after orphans and widows in their distress." God so lovingly cares for those without parents or spouses, in fact, that the primary reason for the tithe explained in Deuteronomy 14:28–29 was so that those without land or inheritance, those without a country, those without fathers, and the widows would "come and eat and be satisfied." We are chosen for Christ to live out this part of our calling to unite as one family, one household, and one body who *cares for the needs of all.*

> WE ARE CHOSEN FOR CHRIST TO LIVE OUT THIS PART OF OUR CALLING TO UNITE AS ONE FAMILY, ONE HOUSEHOLD, AND ONE BODY WHO *CARES FOR THE NEEDS OF ALL.*

This reality solves the problem of our disconnection, loneliness, and longing for that perfect family on the one hand, and it also assigns us a clear task as believers to care for those needing it most. At certain points in your life you might live on the giving side in caring for those in God's family, but most likely you're reading this as someone in desperate need of care from your new family. And as I look back on my life, I'm amazed at how God provided just what I needed in the form of Christians who became my mothers, fathers, sisters and brothers, and even grandparents at points when I needed such care.

Two years ago, for example, God brought me a grandmother of my very own. When we joined a new church two years ago, a silver-haired and rather frail eighty-five-year-old woman at the welcome center asked for my phone number. This precious older woman began calling me nearly every week to make sure I was healthy, happy, and connected to Jesus. My phone would ring, and I'd hear that crackling voice tell me to listen as she read a passage of Scripture just for me. She'd tell me how she loved me and how God was always using us to spread the fragrance of Christ.

After these phone calls, I always felt so loved. I enjoyed the special attention. I treasured the wisdom given. Before I knew what was happening, I realized that God had given me a grandmother. God obviously matched me with my perfect grandmother, too, because she delivers a new book to me nearly every time I see her. She handpicks books for me that she believes will encourage my soul and connect me more with Jesus. If you wonder why I quote A. W. Tozer so much, it's because my church grandmother has given me five of his books! This perfect grandmother not only provides books, but she also invited me as her special guest to our church's regular luncheon for older church members. Yes, I attended the church lunch with a room filled with grandparents. As I loaded my Styrofoam tray with the soft foods that grandparents love—the casseroles, Jell-O salads, and of course, the coconut cakes—and walked slowly through the food line, I listened to my new grandparents teach me about the faithfulness of God throughout a lifetime of trials.

Once, I had no grandparents. Now, I almost have *too many*!

One warm March evening, another elderly couple from church

invited my family to dinner, and a single conversation helped me learn more about the family of God. This couple loves to give our family maple syrup from the trees they tap, and they faithfully pray for us and take a deep interest in our daughters—just as grandparents would. These world travelers settled down in Pennsylvania and cultivated the land around a beautiful home out in the countryside. After hearing about their many travels and all the homes they had lived in, I asked, "Why did you choose to settle here in Pennsylvania? Why, of all the places in the world, would you pick here?" I looked out across the green field where I let my eyes follow a winding creek into the dark forest beyond.

Without even pausing to think, the wife proclaimed, "Because it has the best soil! It has the best soil in the world!"

Something about this statement resonated in my soul as I sat around their big farm table to eat homemade breads and jams and fresh syrup. As I thought about this big family table and looked across at their granddaughter who had stopped by for dinner, I wondered if God wanted to teach me something about His family through that comment about soil from these new grandparent figures in my life.

The next day I emailed my friend Kelly who earned a bachelor's degree in soil science and a master's degree in agronomy from Penn State. She devotes herself to the science of soil management and crop production. I asked Kelly about the idea of "good soil" and what the older woman meant about Pennsylvania soil. I also hoped God was going to teach me something about Himself and my new family.

I asked, "What makes good soil? Is there a spiritual lesson here, too?"

Kelly wrote back something astonishing that I never knew

before. Her words made me feel so sad at first and then so hopeful. She wrote:

> Underneath any soil, there is a layer of rock; we call it bedrock, or *parent* material. The reason we call it the parent material is because as the rock breaks down, soil is formed. In an earthly sense, the parent material is the factor that most influences what type of soil there will be. There are different types of rock, which result in different types of soil, and different properties (or characteristics) of the soil. . . . Whatever the parent material is, that will dictate the soil's properties. Whatever soil a farmer has, he's stuck with it. If I had a clay soil that I wanted more sand in, there's no way I could just change the clay to sand. The main thing is that *the parent bedrock determines the properties of the soil.*[1]

I read Kelly's words, and I felt hopeless for those who have "parent material" that dooms them to a certain kind of life because of abuse, neglect, addiction, or any other reality that harms the well-being of that child as she grows into adulthood. The bedrock determines the soil. That's it. There's no hope. You can't become a different soil.

But then Kelly wrote the most beautiful words:

"But unlike earthly soil, we can choose who our Rock is. Having that is the basis for our whole life—it tells us who we are and what our purpose is."

Jesus is our Rock, our bedrock who replaces our natural family's properties that we wish to change or rise above.

Reading Kelly's words cultivated new gratitude and awe that Jesus rescued us from my parent bedrock—the layer of our life through our ancestors all the way to the original sin of Adam and Eve—and became a new Rock for us. Isn't it wonderful to think of why Jesus is called the Rock so many times in Scripture? We learn that God is called the Rock of Israel (Gen. 49:24), and in Deuteronomy 32:4, we read, "He is the Rock, his works are perfect, and all his ways are just." In fact, in this chapter, this "Song of Moses," Moses calls God "the Rock" five different times, my favorite being when he says, "For their rock is not like our Rock, as even our enemies concede" (v. 31). Hannah's famous prayer in 1 Samuel 2:2 boasts, "There is no Rock like our God." More than thirty more times in the Bible, we see God referred to as our Rock, and in the New Testament, we see Jesus as the rock of our salvation (1 Cor. 10:4). I read that word "rock" and know we have a different foundation, a different bedrock, that determines a new makeup for our lives.

> GOD IS A SOLID FOUNDATION THAT CHANGES THE CONDITIONS OF OUR LIVES—THE PARENT ROCK WHO DETERMINES WHO WE ARE.

God is a solid foundation that changes the conditions of our lives—the Parent Rock who determines who we are.

―∞―

God chooses you to belong to His family. In this family you have the full rights and full inheritance of a treasured son or daughter. In this family the Holy Spirit works to gather us together into deep communion with one another, something only possible by His power.

When God chose you for His family, He intended you to experience the blessing of living in a new household because together we bring glory to Jesus. We are chosen for Christ communally because together we manifest God's presence. You teach me something I didn't know about Jesus just as I showcase something to you that you did not understand before. Our salvation is private and individual, but it's also deeply communal.

Tim Keller, in *The Prodigal God: Recovering the Heart of the Christian Faith*, in the chapter titled, "Salvation Is Communal," explains, "You can't live the Christian life without a band of Christian friends, without a family of believers in which you find a place."[2] What's fascinating isn't that we need this band of friends for ourselves or our own emotional experiences, but because when we're together, *we show one another something special about Jesus*. Keller quotes the famous account in C. S. Lewis's book *The Four Loves*, when Lewis endured the unexpected death of his friend Charles Williams, a member of his literary group, the Inklings. Lewis writes,

> In each of my friends there is something that only some other friend can fully bring out. By myself I am not large enough to call the whole man into activity; I want other lights than my own to show all his facets. Now that Charles is dead, I shall never again see Ronald's [Tolkien's] reaction to a specifically Charles joke. Far from having more of Ronald, having him "to myself" now that Charles is away, I have less of Ronald. . . . In this, Friendship exhibits a glorious "nearness by resemblance" to heaven itself where the very multitude of the blessed (which no man can number) increases the fruition which each of us

W HEN WE'RE TOGETHER, *WE SHOW ONE ANOTHER SOMETHING SPECIAL ABOUT JESUS.*

has of God. For every soul, seeing Him in her own way, doubtless communicates that unique vision to all the rest. That, says an old author, is why the Seraphim in Isaiah's vision are crying "Holy, Holy, Holy" to one another (Isaiah 6:3). The more we thus share the Heavenly Bread between us, the more we shall have.[3]

Lewis explains that with *just one friend missing*, we have less of our other friends because of what that one person could bring out in the others. Lewis compares this experience to our communal experience as Christians because together, we increase what each of us experiences of God. You see Him "in [your] own way" and you communicate that vision to us. Without you, we miss that vision. Keller says it like this: "Lewis is saying that it took a community to know an individual. How much more would this be true of Jesus Christ?"[4]

Can you imagine living as if God chose you for His family because you would communicate a unique vision of Jesus to others —something only you could do, in your way? Can you imagine feeling chosen for this heavenly task that far surpasses any earthly calling? Chosen people—by being authentically ourselves—bring forth something *only we can showcase* of Jesus because of who we are.

So I bring to you verbs and semicolons as I worship God. I bring to you endless curiosity, probing questions, and boundless energy. Maybe, after you leave me, you'll think differently about Jesus through the beauty of vivid verbs—like seated, guarded, included, and chosen.

Maybe I just showed you something you hadn't thought of before.

Because if you were here with me, I'd experience Jesus through you in a special way, a way nobody else but you could show me.

Because chosen women and chosen men know their secure place in the family of God, they now invite others to join this family. I'm no longer that depressed and lonely one always looking for her family. In fact, I now serve as an older sister and mother to anyone who needs to know where they belong. Chosen men and women start each new day with the understanding they have a role in God's household. God chose you, and, as Paul describes in Ephesians 4, *He will use you* to bless your new family.

YOUR NEXT STEP

Read Ephesians 2:19–22.

1. Have you experienced the truth that "God sets the lonely in families"? (Ps. 68:6). Describe those times you felt part of God's household or describe what needs to happen for you to truly feel part of God's family.

2. Write down some of the ways God has redeemed you from the "empty way of life handed down to you" (1 Peter 1:18). These may be sin patterns from your ancestors, beliefs or behaviors of your upbringing, or any ways you felt disconnected from a vibrant, healthy family system. You can even make a chart of "old" and "new" since God is your new "Parent Rock."

3. If you believed that chosen people are called to belong to a new household, how would this change your experience of "family life" every day?

4. Explain the different roles you assume in the family of God. When have you been (or how do you see yourself in the future) like a grandparent, parent, a child, or a sibling?

CHAPTER 8

THE FOURTH INVITATION: COMPLETE GOOD WORKS

*"You did not choose me, but I chose you and appointed you so that
you might go and bear fruit—fruit that will last . . ."*
—JESUS SPEAKING IN JOHN 15:16

When I think about the good works God sets apart for His chosen people, I think of three things: perfume, pumpkins, and pasta.

My children tease me that I hoard perfume samples. It's true. I love perfume. My favorite perfume is Trish McEvoy's No. 9 Blackberry Vanilla Musk that you find only in fancy department stores and never in central Pennsylvania. I felt like a glamorous movie star when I sprayed it on my wrists on a visit to a Nordstrom's in Chicago. My history of perfume dates back to the delicious scent of my mother in her Evening in Paris, her White Shoulders, or her Jovan Musk. As a teen, I wore Love's Baby Soft and the Body Shop's Vanilla Musk, but then I adored Trésor by Lancôme, described as "rose perfume for women that evokes that feeling of everlasting love and makes her as radiant and precious as the fragrance she wears."[1]

As I lived on a missionary budget in my married life, I rarely purchased expensive perfume, so when I visited department stores,

I sprayed my coat and scarf with the $350.00 display sample of Chanel No. 5. I shamelessly coated my sweaters and even my hair with Yves Saint Laurent's Black Opium. I'd shyly ask for any samples to take home because I knew I'd never have the money to afford such luxurious perfumes in their glittering bottles. When Chanel launched Coco Mademoiselle and Gabrielle Chanel, I left stores with whatever samples the salesperson would offer.

What I notice about my perfume is this: I spray it on my body and clothing, and then it does its work. It *wafts*. It somehow combines with my own skin's molecules and releases a unique combination of scent to the world. But I don't do anything. It just works. I never have to say, "Now fragrance, start working! Go!" No, it just produces the scent as I go about my day.

I think about fragrance because of a passage of Scripture I adore. In 2 Corinthians 2:14–15 we read this: "But thanks be to God, who in Christ always leads us in triumphal procession, and through us spreads the fragrance of the knowledge of him everywhere. For we are the aroma of Christ to God among those who are being saved and among those who are perishing" (ESV). God spreads everywhere we go the fragrance of Christ. To God, we smell like Jesus.

Isn't that so amazing? I wonder what Jesus smells like and how I smell like Him. Throughout Exodus, Leviticus, and Numbers we learn that the burnt offerings to the Lord were a "pleasing aroma" to Him. The acceptable sacrifice became a pleasing aroma in the Old Testament, and now Jesus becomes the final, pleasing atoning sacrifice for sin. The "aroma of Christ" we read about reminds us of the burnt offering for sin.

In the New Testament, the sacrifice isn't burnt, but it's *broken*. We know from Isaiah 53 that the Savior is "crushed for our iniquities" (v. 5) and that we take His body that is broken for us when we take communion (1 Cor. 11:24). Burning and crushing *release fragrance.* I remember this when I feel crushed by difficult circumstances. Picture how we crush and rub fresh herbs in order to release their aroma and flavor while cooking. When I feel the pressure of my daily tasks or any fears I'm facing, I think of releasing that beautiful aroma of Christ because I'm worshiping Him and relying on His power right here. As I think about the concept of fragrance, I imagine myself walking around and, just as my perfume exudes that distinct scent, my life exudes something about Jesus that people *can sense.*

Several times in my life someone has approached me to tell me they "sense something" different about me. When they say this, I find myself in awe of the changes He has made in me and the work God has done to make someone as lost as I was more like Jesus. People have even asked me if I take a special drug. They ask if I have some secret to happiness and joy. How can I stay so cheerful when life feels so hard?

I tell them that they are sensing the presence of the Living God, Jesus Christ, who indwells me by the Holy Spirit. If someone asks about my perfume, I tell them without hesitation that it's Gabrielle Chanel, so I'm learning more to name the happiness others sense in me as Jesus Christ.

PERFUME DOES ITS WORK, AND WE DON'T HAVE TO FORCE IT. WHEN WE THINK ABOUT THE GOOD WORKS GOD PREPARED IN ADVANCE FOR US TO DO, WE CAN REMEMBER PERFUME'S INEVITABLE WORK. WE CAN APPLY THE RIGHTEOUSNESS OF CHRIST LIKE FRAGRANCE.

Perfume does its work, and we don't have to force it. When

we think about the good works God prepared in advance for us to do, we can remember perfume's inevitable work. We can apply the righteousness of Christ like fragrance. I move out into my day in the hope, joy, and power of the Holy Spirit, and I know I'm radiating something of Jesus. I imagine God "making his appeal through [me]" (2 Cor. 5:20) to others, just like fragrance emanating from my body.

I trust God to use me like this. I know that He "always leads" me to spread the fragrance of Christ. I stand confident in evangelism for this reason: I know God is leading me and using me to reflect Him somehow. He chose me to become the fragrance of Christ to attract people to Him.

You need to know something else about me. I'm not just a perfume sample hoarder. I'm a pumpkin farmer. I've been coaxing my neighbors into the backyard to observe the most extraordinary phenomenon in the garden. First of all, I never imagined I'd be the kind of woman who lures people behind the house to insist they admire her vegetables and fruit, but here I am. Second, I was supposed to live a glamorous life in some big city, but God settled me down in a small neighborhood in central Pennsylvania where, besides learning how to compost, I once used a tiny hammer to crack open hundreds of acorns from the oaks in my yard to get to the inner nutmeat, which I then leached for four hours in boiling water so I could grind the nutmeat into acorn flour. Yes, I've become a person who uses verbs like *compost* and *leach*.

When the neighbors turn the corner, they bump into a pumpkin patch so big, they put their hands over their mouths and actually gasp. Six pumpkins, the size of television sets, blaze orange against the green of my lawn and the blue of the autumn sky. "Can you believe it?" I ask.

"What happened? How did this ever happen? I didn't know you knew how to do this," my neighbor says.

"Stand right here," I insist. "I have to tell you what God is teaching me through my pumpkins!"

I then point to my compost pile that sits against the brown fence that nobody can even see through the pumpkin leaves. Deep in the compost, a single vine grows. In that compost bin, my husband piled grass clippings, weeds, egg shells, coffee grounds, the rinds of fruits and vegetables, and paper towels. He uses a pitchfork to mix the trash with the moist soil. Then, microorganisms do the work of decomposition to gift us with nutrient rich soil.

"It's the garbage of my life," I explain. "You're looking at the disaster of decomposing, lost things." I explain that in the garbage of my life, I tossed decaying pumpkins last year, the one my daughters carved into owls and cats. We returned from a trip to Colorado this past summer to find an enormous vine, from a *single seed*, overtaking the yard. Planted in the destruction that compost represents—which happens to be the best fertilizer—the pumpkin vine grew. I never tended it. I never did anything.

I point to the largest pumpkin. "See what God can do when we allow the smallest seed of faith to take root in our lives, no matter how messed up we are? See what God can do in the garbage of our lives? Trust Him! When you sow to please the Spirit, you will reap the most glorious harvest!"

My neighbors nod, and sometimes their eyes fill with tears. As they experience the heat of decomposition—through divorce, illness, job transitions, wayward children, or any host of difficult events—they see how a single, tiny turning toward God in faith—as small as a pumpkin seed—allows the Holy Spirit to work a harvest right there in what they perceive as the garbage of life.

I think of Jesus insisting to me over and over again: "I chose you and appointed you so that you might go and bear fruit—fruit that will last" (John 15:16). I think of Psalm 1 and the promise to those who meditate on God's words and how they live like a tree that "yields its fruit in season and whose leaf does not wither—whatever they do prospers." My pumpkin patch daily reminds me that, no matter what my present situation, God can and will bring a harvest of His presence and His abundant life right here. He can produce the fruit of good character and the fruit of leading others to Christ and helping them grow.

My horticulturalist friends (yes, I have *horticulturalists* as friends instead of celebrities or socialites like I once wanted) helped me understand something so essential with one simple question last month, back when I didn't know what kind of vine I had growing from my compost bin. What in the world was that thing? Was I growing watermelons? Squash? Zucchini? Some mutant vine that would take over the house?

"Well," my horticulturalist friend asks slowly, "what did you throw into your compost?"

What did I put in there? I thought of my own heart and what seeds I'm planting there. Whatever I plant will grow and produce fruit, whether bitterness and evil or joy and righteousness. "I suppose I threw my old jack-o-lanterns in there last November when the snow came. They were just shriveled and rotting away. But I had removed all the seeds and roasted them."

"It just takes one seed."

As I look carefully at John 15:1–5, I learn something else vital about Jesus and this concept of producing fruit. Fruit producing comes about through *pruning* and *nourishment from the right source*. Jesus says:

> I am the true vine, and my Father is the gardener. He cuts off every branch in me that bears no fruit, while every branch that does bear fruit he prunes so that it will be even more fruitful. You are already clean because of the word I have spoken to you. Remain in me, as I also remain in you. No branch can bear fruit by itself; it must remain in the vine. Neither can you bear fruit unless you remain in me. I am the vine; you are the branches. If you remain in me and I in you, you will bear much fruit; apart from me you can do nothing.

Here, I learn to see myself as a branch extending from Jesus as my Vine. The parts of me that don't bear fruit, He cuts off *so that I might be more fruitful*. I think of seasons of pruning that we experience as loss: the cooling of relationships, losing a job, moving to a new location, the diminishing of activities or even ministry work, or any other kind of ending. What feels like something cut off in us might actually function as the means by which God makes us more fruitful. God is always working to bear fruit through us. As Jesus says, "This is to my Father's glory, that you bear much fruit" (John 15:8). When God removes something or someone from our life, ends an activity, or changes our location, we can remember His pruning work is to *make us more fruitful*. He chooses us to bear much fruit. Jesus even reiterates that He chose us and also "appointed" us to bear fruit (v. 16).

Can you imagine feeling chosen and appointed—ordained, set apart for specific assignments—rather than feeling outside of God's plan for your life? Doesn't it feel so secure and clear to know that God has chosen and appointed you for the activities of your life?

Resting in God's chosen and appointed plan for me to bear fruit settles my heart down when I'm scrambling for achievement, comparing my work to others, or worried that I've somehow missed God's plan for me. And you can rest in this knowledge too!

Perfume and pumpkins teach me to apply His righteousness and abide in Christ to bear fruit. And now, one more image has cemented my chosen identity as someone set apart for good works.

I recently enjoyed dinner with a large Italian family in New Jersey who hosted me for a speaking event. A tiny moment happened at this dinner that revealed something special to me about Jesus. While my friendship with Italian mothers in my neighborhood in Pennsylvania had offered me comprehensive training in what to expect from Italian family dinners, nothing prepared me for the meal that night.[2]

This Italian gathering wasn't simply abundant with delicious foods like chicken piccata, creamy risotto, thick slices of crusty Italian bread, chopped salad with fresh oregano and basil, and the promise of rich coffee and desserts afterwards, but it also positioned me in the middle of a lively and animated discussion.

Italians talk. They talk loudly. They love hand gestures and enthusiastic expressions. At this table, besides me, were grandparents, two teen brothers, a father and mother, and a daughter no more than six years old, all competing for attention. We all had *so much to say*. As we talked over one another, interrupting, laughing, and adding on to the comment just said before, I noticed something that pierced my heart.

The young daughter, so small she sat on her knees to reach the plate before her, tried to make her voice heard. She tried to enter into the conversation, but with everyone speaking over her, her face grew more and more frustrated with furrowed brows and a frown. I wondered if she would burst into tears, but instead she snuck out of her seat, tiptoed over to her Italian father at the head of the table next to me, pulled on his arm until he leaned down to her face, and whispered these words to him.

"Daddy, I cannot find my space. There's no space for me to say what I need to say. I cannot find my space."

I cannot find my space here.

The Italian father lifted his great hand into the air and silenced us all. He said, "This little one has something to say to us."

In the silence, as the child stood by her father, she informed us all of her monumental news: she had a loose tooth. Then she returned to her seat.

Days later—even months later—I replayed the scene in my mind. Something about that little girl who couldn't make her voice heard—who couldn't contribute in the midst of so much activity and noise—made me think of all of us clamoring to use our gifts. We have something to say, but we cannot find our space. We have something to offer, but it often feels like nobody's listening. The noise of others and all their books and blogs and social media posts makes it feel like, although we're still seated at the table, we don't have anything to say here that people would ever hear.

Until you talk to the Father about it.

WATCHING THE FATHER LIFT HIS AUTHORITATIVE HAND TO MAKE SPACE FOR THAT LITTLE GIRL SHOWED ME SOMETHING ABOUT GOD. GOD MAKES SPACE FOR US TO USE OUR GIFTS.

Watching the Italian father lift his authoritative hand to make space for that little girl showed me something about God. God makes space for us to use our gifts. He knows how to open doors, use our gifting, and make our contribution matter. When we feel crowded out, Jesus is right there, appointing and enabling the fruit for our lives. He's clearing ground and making a way for us to bear fruit and to complete the good works He has prepared in advance for us to do (Eph. 2:10).

Jesus is helping us find our space to display the good works He chooses for us. If you are a young person reading this, consider how God clears space for you. Consider your life as the compost into which you plant seeds, day after day, to become more like Jesus and one day bear the fruit He's planned for you. Consider the reality that God is using you to radiate the fragrance of Christ. And when you feel fruitless, confused, and without a goal, consider Pastor Neil Anderson's words: "It should be obvious by now that God's basic goal for your life is character development: become the person God wants you to be. Sanctification is God's goal for your life. . . . Nobody and nothing on planet Earth can keep you from being the person God called you to be."[3]

You don't have to wait. You can begin today to step into the life you've been missing by allowing God to shape your character. You can begin today to "keep in step with the Spirit" and you'll find that, over time, your life will *bear fruit.* Your character will show in increasing measure the fruit of the Spirit described in Galatians

5:22–23 (ESV): "love, joy, peace, patience, kindness, goodness, faithfulness, gentleness, self-control." You'll also find encouragement in the words Paul used in Galatians 6:9: "Let us not become weary in doing good, for at the proper time we will reap a harvest if we do not give up." What is this harvest? The blessing of doing the works He gave us, seeing our character grow to become more like Him, enriching God's kingdom as we love and serve others . . . and, of special blessing, the harvest of new believers, all of which will fill your heart with indescribable joy.

———

Perfume, pumpkins, and pasta remind me that I'm chosen to bear fruit.

You will bear fruit. This will happen. Hannah Whitall Smith assures us: "God's purpose in our salvation is that we should bring forth fruit. A husbandman plants the vine for the sake of the grapes it will bear; the farmer plants his apple orchard for the sake of the apples it will bear; the farmer plants his apple orchard in order to gather fruit; Christ has chosen us that we should bring forth fruit. A fruitless Christian life is an impossibility."[4]

A fruitless Christian life is an impossibility.

———

As you move into your day, think of these words to summarize your chosen identity. Paul writes in Philippians 1:25–26: "I will remain and continue with you all, for your progress and joy in the faith, so that in me you may have ample cause to glory in Christ Jesus, because of my coming to you again" (ESV). Imagine your friends and family saying that your presence causes their joy in Jesus to increase. Imagine your purpose as a chosen person includes aiding the progress and joy of the faith journeys of those around you.

Chosen people cause others to rejoice in Jesus. They help others progress in their faith and add to their joy in the Lord.

Chosen men and women lead the way into the life of Christ by journeying alongside others and inviting them into this chosen life they've been missing. And I can give you a physical, if rather awkward, image of what we do as chosen people.

I was speaking at a women's retreat in the South, and the ministry director wanted to create a special moment for women to come kneel before the Lord at the altar. She hoped they would enjoy a moment of prayer to offer themselves afresh to Jesus. But we feared that nobody would ever do this. It's too public, too embarrassing, and too awkward to walk down the aisle in front of everyone, then kneel down and pray.

"What if I went first?" I offered. "What if I told the women that I would kneel down before the Lord, offer myself anew, and pray about my children, work, and neighbors? What if I told them to come along—that they wouldn't be alone—and that I would show them how?"

As I ended my presentation and the worship leader strummed her guitar, I told the women what I was going to do. I said, "I know it's hard to make a public declaration before the Lord, to surrender to Him in a significant way that others witness, but I will do it first. You can follow me."

I hobbled down the steps to the platform, turned around, and flung my body down to kneel—only to remember my bad knee doesn't allow me to kneel. So in a half bent position, I rolled over onto my side like a beached whale with my rear end pointing out. Or picture a great ship keeling over.

There I was.

And there, spread out in front of all those women, I closed my eyes and silently prayed that God would take over every part of my life for His purposes. At first I thought the plan had failed; I *was* a beached whale, a ship keeled over, a woman with bad knees making a fool of herself. But then I began to hear movement as woman after woman came forward to kneel before the Lord. They all knelt down beside me—too many to count—as they talked to Jesus themselves, some for the very first time. They prayed. They wept. They consecrated themselves.

They just needed someone to go before them, to show them how.

YOUR NEXT STEP

—⟋⟍—

Read 2 Corinthians 2:14–17.

1. What does it mean to you that, like perfume others can smell, God is using you to spread the "fragrance of Christ"?

2. Describe a time when a small turning toward God produced fruit in your life like a pumpkin seed in compost.

3. Are you in a season of asking God to help you find your space for ministry? Record your thoughts of where this "space" might be. How do you sense the Lord leading you?

4. Where in your ministry to others do you need to model what it means to surrender to the Lord?

CHAPTER 9

THE FIFTH INVITATION: DISPLAY GOD'S POWER

You answer us with awesome and righteous deeds, God our Savior.
—DAVID IN PSALM 65:5a

The Lord may not come when you call, but He's always on time.
—POET AND SPOKEN WORD ARTIST LEMON ANDERSON

When I was in middle school I began the practice of recording my prayers in a lined notebook with a stubby pencil. I talked to Jesus as I read my burgundy *Children's Good News Bible* on my lap. Scripture began to come alive for me; I felt the comforting presence of the Holy Spirit, especially as I read the Psalms. In that bedroom I felt seen and chosen. I knew two things for sure as I sat in flowered pajamas by the window that overlooked the Potomac River: God loved me. And God was powerful.

I hid the notebook underneath the sweaters in a drawer (in the same oak dresser that sits in my own daughter's bedroom now thirty years later) and recorded my secret requests. I scribbled my prayers in urgent lists, and I left room on the page to record when and how God answered my prayer. I still recall those prayers that ranged from asking God to heal a sick family member to giving me courage to talk about Jesus at the school lunch table. I wrote down prayers about my cats, tests, and friends who were fighting with their parents.

I believed God answered prayer, so I prayed to Him then just as I do now. And my own daughter has a morning prayer journal to record her own heart's concerns to the same Jesus who loves and sees her.

Nothing has built my faith more—besides reading God's Word—than seeing God's powerful activity in response to prayer. In Jeremiah 33:3, we see the great promise of God, "Call to me and I will answer you . . ." In Hebrews 4:16, we know we "approach the throne of grace with confidence, so that we may receive mercy and find grace to help us in our time of need." In Psalm 65:2, David calls God, "You who answer prayer."

I shared Psalm 5:3 with our daughters recently, and I repeat it often before we leave the house in the morning. David says, "In the morning, LORD, you hear my voice; in the morning I lay my requests before you and wait expectantly."

Besides our private prayer journals, our family displays a special golden jar of rocks in our living room with an ornate prayer journal beside it. When God answers a family prayer, we put a rock into the jar. Our family jar of stones represents those moments when God answered prayer in a particularly powerful way—whether healing a very sick child, providing financially, or opening the door to a special opportunity.

We do this because of Joshua 4:4–7 where God parts the Jordan River so the Israelites can pass safely. When the miracle occurred, Joshua instructs the people to take up stones of remembrance of the miracle. He explains that this would "serve as a sign among you. In the future, when your children ask you, 'What do these stones mean?' tell them that the flow of the Jordan was cut off before the ark of the covenant of the LORD. When it crossed the Jordan, the waters of the Jordan were cut off. These stones are to be a memorial to the people of Israel forever." The stones commemorated a display of God's power.

In that jar we have a stone to remember the day I prayed about finding a house to live in on our missionary budget. One winter day after prayer, I felt the Lord call to mind a person who I knew had a large home he often rented out in a beautiful neighborhood of professors. I asked my husband to call that man even though it was the day before Christmas Eve and such a strange time to make a phone call about a house. When my husband called the man, he said, "I cannot believe your timing! My renters just left for another job in New York, and I need some renters."

My husband pulled up the picture of the house on the internet based on the address and sadly said, "That's wonderful, but this home is beautiful and larger than we could ever afford to rent. We thought we'd call just to find out about it."

The man said, "What can you afford?"

My husband explained that we were missionaries with Cru, and we served graduate students on campus to help them know Jesus. The man said in disbelief that he was a Christian who years ago was involved in the *very same ministry to graduate students that we were now directing.* He was thrilled that his home might be used to bless graduate students through the ministry he loved.

My husband paused, and the man said, "What are you paying for rent now?" We were living in a tiny, rundown home across town. "I want you to pay that rent—the price you can afford."

For eight years we lived in an enormous home, paying a measly rent. When the time came for the man to sell that beautiful home, I prayed again that God would make a way for us to buy that house.

It was an impossible prayer. We would never have the money for a down payment. We would never own such a fine home as this.

But I prayed. I asked God for a *house*.

And again, the man said, "What can you afford?"

We bought that house with the help of ministry partners and this owner who negotiated a price we could afford. We're living in that house now. And there's a big stone in my prayer jar of remembrance.

—⚏—

Other stones represent the provision of medical care, the repairing of relationships, and the movement of God to provide new opportunities in writing books, speaking, and serving in new ways as missionaries. One stone represents the day I cried out to God to provide a minivan for us because our old van was breaking down. We needed a way to drive to Colorado for our summer missions conference. "Jesus," I cried. "We need transportation!" That evening, a man from our church called and said he was trying to donate to charity a company car—a sturdy burgundy Honda minivan. Did we know of anyone who needed a *free minivan*?

I'm certain that if you began a collection of your own stones of remembrance, you too would have a jarful. By now, our stories of answered prayer feel too vast to recount. I know the love of God to answer prayers and display His power, and it thrills me to think that I can come to Jesus with any concern or any need, and He hears and answers in His way, in His timing, for my good and for His glory.

—⚏—

I'm sitting in church, and I hear the worship leader invite us to call out to Jesus. She then says, "and He will come *swiftly*." I immediately thought of Isaiah 30:19 where the prophet comforts God's people with this promise: "People of Zion, who live in Jerusalem, you will weep no more. How gracious he will be when you cry for help! As soon as he hears, he will answer you." I think of how swiftly Jesus comes and how "as soon as he hears" He begins to answer. I also considered Isaiah 65:24 where, in the New Living Translation, we learn this about God: "I will answer them before they even call to me. While they are still talking about their needs, I will go ahead and answer their prayers!" When I think of God treating me like this to answer prayers I haven't even asked yet, I'm filled with awe, peace, and comfort. Why would I worry about anything if God could display His power like this on my behalf?

―⟋⟍―

God displays His power throughout the Bible in many miraculous ways in the Old Testament—through creation, the flood, the parting of the Red Sea, the provision of manna and quail while the Israelites wandered in the desert, and the dramatic scene of fire coming down from heaven in the presence of the prophets of Baal in 1 Kings 18 (to name only a few).

In the New Testament we observe this same God of power through the birth of Christ from a virgin, the miracles performed by Jesus—including healing the sick, the demon possessed, and the paralyzed, commanding nature, and changing and multiplying the elements of wine and food. Some of the miracles of Jesus are so delightful because they seem whimsical, like when Jesus tells the disciples to catch a fish that happens to have a coin in its mouth to pay the taxes they owe (Matt. 17:27) or how he feeds over five thousand people with a little boy's lunch (Matt. 14:13–21).

We serve a God of loving, personal, incredible power that

becomes available to us as Christians. In fact, when you read of our chosen identity in Ephesians, you'll find that Paul immediately instructs us about our power as chosen people. Consider Ephesians 1:19–20a and Paul's prayer that we would now know "his incomparably great power for us who believe. That power is the same as the mighty strength he exerted when he raised Christ from the dead." Can you imagine? What if we lived as if the power that raised Christ from the dead—all that power never limited by nature, resources, time, or any kind of physical reality we understand—truly operated within us? So important is our knowledge of this power that Paul asks God again for us who believe—you and me— that He would "strengthen you with power through his Spirit in your inner being" (Eph. 3:16).

In case we were confused about the importance of maintaining a clear understanding of this available power, Paul ends his letter to the Ephesians by saying, "Finally, be strong in the Lord and in his mighty power" (6:10). We have *power* as God's chosen people. We have the power described long ago in Isaiah 40:29: "He gives strength to the weary and increases the power of the weak."

W E HAVE *POWER* AS GOD'S CHOSEN PEOPLE. WE HAVE THE POWER DESCRIBED LONG AGO IN ISAIAH 40:29: "HE GIVES STRENGTH TO THE WEARY AND INCREASES THE POWER OF THE WEAK."

When you think about what chosen people need power for, or if you wonder how God intends to display His power through you and within this ordinary day, we can look to the Bible to tell us.

Chosen people have *power to defeat the enemy*. Jesus informs us explicitly when He sends out messengers in Luke 10. He says,

"I have given you authority . . . to overcome all the power of the enemy" (v. 19). The power of the enemy comes against us in many forms: confusion, dread, illness, accusation, lies, temptation, harassment, and diversion from our calling. If you search the Scriptures to recount how Satan works, you'll observe these predictable attacks. You'll begin to recognize this work in your own life—but because of the Holy Spirit's power, you take your stand against the enemy. You win against this "lion looking for someone to devour" (1 Peter 5:8). God allows a defeated enemy to come against us because He's teaching us something; we experience these things so we know the power we have in Jesus' name. How would I know Jesus' power over evil if I never encountered that "lion"?

This year, as I experienced God's deliverance from what felt like an oppressive spirit of dread and confusion over me, I knew to thank Him for allowing me to feel demonic activity *so I would know His power to overcome it.* I know how to recognize despair and accusation from Satan because I've experienced it firsthand. And God, as a faithful and good teacher, instructs me how to stand in the truth of God's Word and in my identity as a chosen daughter when I feel under spiritual attack.

—⁂—

Chosen people also live *as agents of proclamation*, entrusted with the power to call spiritually dead people back to life. In Acts 1:8, Jesus teaches that "you will receive power when the Holy Spirit comes on you; and you will be my witnesses." When people ask me how I became an evangelist, I tell them that once you experience the power of God to change someone's life, you're never the same. That supernatural adventure and joy of working alongside Jesus to seek the lost begins to shape everything you do.

I leave the house in the full power of the Holy Spirit to live as a witness, to fish for people, and to be a worker where the "harvest is plentiful" (Matt. 9:37). I do not go out as a laborer in my own power; I know God empowers me through His Holy Spirit to draw people to Jesus and lead them to salvation. I experience this power when God leads me to people, when He gives me words to say to them, and when I see a person respond to the gospel. I know God has given me "divine power to demolish strongholds" (2 Cor. 10:4), so I move about my day in prayer that God would take down any stronghold keeping a person's heart from responding to God.

—⁓—

Chosen people also allow the Holy Spirit to empower them to *live above their circumstances* and fill them with the fruit of the Spirit (Gal. 5). We can live as people of love, joy, peace, patience, kindness, goodness, gentleness, faithfulness, and self-control. But in order to teach us to live in this power, God often brings us to people and places that require supernatural character. As you think about your life, consider the following:

> *What people in your life require God's power for you to love them?*
>
> *What robs you of joy?*
>
> *What trouble steals your peace?*
>
> *Which people need kindness that's hard to offer?*
>
> *Where can you bring goodness?*
>
> *Who tests your patience?*
>
> *When do you want to react harshly instead of with gentleness?*

What circumstances currently require faithfulness?
Where do you lack self-control?

As you fill out this list, consider how the Holy Spirit will increasingly produce this "fruit" of good character in your life. It's so exciting to think about what kind of person you'll be in just a year. Now imagine five years. Now imagine a decade. What if God truly shaped you into a person who loves the unlovable, finds joy anywhere, exudes peace, offers kindness and goodness at all times, and exhibits patience, gentleness, and faithfulness?

And what if you finally lived a disciplined, self-controlled life, especially in the areas of overeating, overspending, or overindulging in anything that controls your heart?

This power doesn't depend on your earning it, begging for it, or somehow hoping it will work for you. Our daily expectation as chosen people changes; we know God's power works within us because of Jesus Christ and what He has accomplished in forgiving our sins and clothing us with His righteousness. We appropriate the power of the Holy Spirit on that basis, not because we somehow deserve it.

—◊◊—

Chosen people display God's power despite their weakness, flaws, and continued struggle with sin. They live lives characterized by God's strength, not their own. They live in His power, not their own. They proclaim like Paul in Philippians 4:13: "I can do all this through him who gives me strength." Scripture teaches us that God displays His power through our lives in ways that bring Him glory and honor because we're in situations *that require supernatural power*. In 2 Corinthians 12:9 we see this principle of wanting to rise above human weakness—to be strong in ourselves—and God responding like this: "My grace is sufficient for you, for my power is made perfect in weakness" and Paul saying, "Therefore I will boast all the more gladly about my weaknesses, so that Christ's power may rest on me." In fact, Paul didn't boast in his human strength; he continued to boast in his weakness so Christ would receive glory, not himself (2 Cor. 11:30).

Paul even says he delights "in weaknesses . . . in hardships . . . in difficulties" (2 Cor. 12:10). Can you imagine *delighting* in your weaknesses, hardships, and difficulties? What if you truly believed God brought you to the very situation you dread because God intends to display His power right there? What if we understood that God brought us to places of need and powerlessness so we could know with certainty that "God is our refuge and strength, an ever-present help in trouble" (Ps. 46:1)?

And the beautiful truth is this:

> *We'll know it's God's power because we're so weak,*
> *broken, and unworthy that it must be Him.*

If you look through the Bible, you'll find, from beginning to end, a radical dependence on God's power displayed in weak, ordinary lives. Moses and Miriam proclaim in song to the Lord, "The LORD is my strength and my defense; he has become my salvation" (Ex. 15:2), and we see Moses declaring, "May the Lord's strength be displayed" (Num. 14:17). As we move through the Scriptures, we see how David learns how to "find strength in the LORD his God" (1 Sam. 30:6).

Where do you need His strength today? Where do you need a demonstration of the Holy Spirit's power? What feels like a "wall" blocking you from doing what you feel called to do? In 2 Samuel 22 David writes, "The LORD turns my darkness into light. With your help I can advance against a troop; with my God I can scale a wall. . . . It is God who arms me with strength and keeps my way secure. He makes my feet like the feet of a deer; he causes me to stand on the heights" (vv. 29–34).

WHERE DO YOU NEED HIS STRENGTH TODAY? WHERE DO YOU NEED A DEMONSTRATION OF THE HOLY SPIRIT'S POWER? WHAT FEELS LIKE A "WALL" BLOCKING YOU FROM DOING WHAT YOU FEEL CALLED TO DO?

We can advance against a troop of discouraging news. We can scale a wall of what seems like impossible tasks. We can stand on the heights over our dismal circumstances.

God wants to meet you in those moments of perceived defeat and display His power. He proclaims, "I am with you; do not be dismayed, for I am your God. I will strengthen you and help you; I will uphold you with my righteous right hand" (Isa. 41:10).

Chosen people live as a display of *God's power*. Chosen people experience the weakness, difficulty, and hardship of life but simultaneously live in Christ's power. God always works in these ways; He always works to display His power. In Psalm 77:14 we read, "You are the God who performs miracles; you display your power among the peoples."

Finally, if we believe God chooses our circumstances because He will display His power there, we approach our days as expectant observers and learners. Make it a habit to ask, "What am I learning about Jesus' power through this event or this person?" This power might appear as an answer to prayer, sending you as an agent of proclamation, or as the power to live with the fruit of the Spirit when a situation tests your love, joy, peace, patience, kindness, gentleness, faithfulness, and self-control.

When I'm in a discouraging situation, I ask, "God, how will you display your power here?" My husband reminded me of one of the best questions to ask in a mentoring setting or with people experiencing pain or frustration in their lives. He asks, "How are you experiencing God's power in this situation?" You can be sure that, whatever happens to you today, God will use it to teach you more about His power.

God is a Good Teacher. Over forty-three times in the New Testament we see Jesus referred to as a *teacher*. In Psalm 71:17 the psalmist says, "Since my youth, God, you have taught me, and to this day I declare your marvelous deeds." God intends to teach you through the experiences of your ordinary day to show you more of Himself. When your life doesn't make sense, and it seems like God has come too late, remember that God's timing is always right. You're right where you are because, as God's chosen, He will display His power on your behalf.

YOUR NEXT STEP

—⁓—

1. Start a prayer journal and begin writing down your prayer requests and then wait with expectation.

2. In what areas of your life do you find yourself most weary and in need of God's strength?

3. What aspects of God's power in your life most excite you: His answers to prayer, His divine appointments for you, or His transformation of your character?

4. Describe a time when you experienced God's power in your life in any form. What do you think keeps people from experiencing God's power more regularly?

—ɯ—

THE SIXTH INVITATION: BECOME LIKE JESUS

*But there is no use in trying to engraft an opposite nature
on one's own. What I am, that I must be, except as God changes
me into His own image. And everything brings me back
to that, as my supreme desire.*

—ELIZABETH PRENTISS, *STEPPING HEAVENWARD*

*For those God foreknew he also predestined to be
conformed to the image of his Son.*

—ROMANS 8:29a

This past Sunday I found myself uncomfortably waddling in a scratchy yellow robe with a burgundy sash as I held a giant stuffed Dalmatian dog. I stepped onto the stage of our church's children ministry room to fill the role of storyteller for the month. I dressed as Abraham and carried that dog as a prop to help me tell the story of Abraham giving his nephew Lot the "good land" because Abraham could trust God to provide for him.

The kindergartners fought to pet my Dalmatian. The third graders were confused why my "good land" props included a bean bag and historically inaccurate plastic food like pancake mix and sushi.

The fourth graders thought I looked more like Moses. "It's Moses! It's Moses!" they shouted until I corrected them. The fifth graders called out, "Isn't Lot in Sodom?" I had failed to bring props for Sodom.

What am I doing up here, Lord?

I tried my best.

In the chaos and confusion, the laughter and all my nervous insecurity, I glanced over that room of squirming children, and I recalled the day I agreed to join this team of children's ministry workers because I had just learned something so important about Jesus. I had learned that God chose me "to be conformed to the image of his Son."

The week before, I skimmed the Gospels to answer the questions "What is Jesus *really* like? How does He *actually* behave? If God is making me more like Jesus, what's that going to look like in a practical way?"

And I couldn't deny it: Jesus cares deeply about children.

Jesus adores children. He blesses them. He wants them around Him (Luke 18:15–17). I wasn't prepared for how bad this made me feel about my own journey to become more like Jesus. I don't love children like He does. Since our own daughters have grown to teens, I find myself thankfully spending less and less time with small children. I remember those early parenting days as labor intensive, loud, and a never-ending, sticky battle to clean up after them. I tense up when babies cry or toddlers begin to fuss. I find my heart growing more indifferent to the needs of these precious souls that Jesus explicitly adores.

The next night a family with young children came to our house for dinner, and I wanted so much to have Jesus change my attitude and heart about loving and blessing children. Could the Holy Spirit draw me again to children to love and care for them as He does?

I had just read Jesus' instructions about children and that they have special "angels in heaven" Matthew 18:10: "See that you do not despise one of these little ones. For I tell you that their angels in heaven always see the face of my Father in heaven." I thought about Jesus wanting the children to come to Him so He could bless them (Matt. 19:14), and I felt a fresh love well up within me. I pictured Jesus placing His hands on the little children and speaking a special blessing over each one. I thought of the strange and beautiful concept that children have angels who gaze upon God.

Children matter to Jesus profoundly.

As I was thinking about these things, I received an email from the children's ministry director at our church to ask me if I would please serve as the Sunday school storyteller *for the children* in March. It felt strange, out of the blue, and intended for another Heather.

Me? Are you sure? But I'm a college instructor. I'm a mom of teens. Everyone knows I'm impatient with children and have become a rusty, crusty, irritable person with those little ones! Not me! You've contacted the wrong Heather.

But God moved in that moment. God was preparing my heart as I prepared to write this very chapter to receive an invitation to bless children.

Yes, I'll be your storyteller. Yes, I'll bless the children.

I know I'm chosen for Christ to become like the Son who loved and cared for children, and this represents just one way my chosen identity takes on the likeness of Jesus.

———∿∿———

As I stepped into this new, extraordinary life that so far invites me to live as chosen for Jesus—to somehow make His name great and to fulfill this purpose for which I was made—I found myself thrilled to think that this "new me" lived this very day as a worshiper, as a treasured possession, and as belonging to a new family.

Instead of self-exaltation, I now worship God in new ways.

Instead of uncertain of God's tender care for me, I live as His treasured possession with a joyful expectation of daily demonstrations of His love.

Instead of dwelling in loneliness and disconnection, I belong to a new family, complete good works, and display His power.

And then I realized *it gets even better.*

In Romans 8:29 we read that God chooses us to become like His Son. Paul describes this new sense of identity best in Galatians 1:15–16. He writes that God set him "apart from my mother's womb" and called Paul by His grace, "to reveal his Son" in him so Paul could fulfill the tasks for which God had called him.

God wants to reveal His Son in us.

The most beautiful journey of our Christian lives isn't personal ministry, impact, prosperity, or happiness. It's the privilege of *becoming more and more like Jesus* because of the power of the Holy Spirit. We're told in Scripture that Christians put on a "new self, created to be like God in righteousness and holiness" (Eph. 4:24). We're told in Ephesians 5:1–2 (esv) something about what our lives might look like: "Therefore be imitators of God, as beloved children. And walk in love, as Christ loved us and gave himself up for us, a fragrant offering and sacrifice to God."

> THE GOAL OF OUR CHOSEN IDENTITY CENTERS ON ALLOWING THE HOLY SPIRIT TO MAKE US MORE LIKE JESUS.

Walk in love.

Give yourself up.

I want to walk in love. I want to love like Jesus and give myself up for others like Jesus. The entire goal of my life no longer orbits around fame, influence, money, achievement, comfort, or even personal happiness. The goal of my chosen identity centers on allowing the Holy Spirit to make me more like Jesus.

—〰—

Before delving into all we might observe about what it means to become like Jesus, let's first note the prime importance of such a life goal. Elizabeth Prentiss, in her 1869 diary that became the beloved classic *Stepping Heavenward*, expresses that becoming transformed "into His own image" is now her "supreme desire."[1]

Theologian Richard Foster's article "Becoming Like Christ," published in *Christianity Today*, tells us "the daring goal of the Christian life could be summarized as our being formed, conformed, and transformed into the image of Jesus Christ."[2] This "daring goal" of becoming like Jesus often falls to the background of our lives as we seek relationship satisfaction, career success, and ministry impact. We forget that God chose us *to become like His Son.*

John Stott, the Christian leader ranked by *Time* magazine in 2005 as one of the 100 most influential people in the world,[3] delivered a final address in which he attempts to answer the question "What is God's purpose for His people?" Stott wrestled with the ultimate goal, the best purpose he could proclaim to us, and said this, "I want to share with you where my mind has come to rest as I approach the end of my pilgrimage on earth, and it is— God wants His people to become like Christ. Christlikeness is the will of God for the people of God."[4]

I want to become *more and more like Jesus*. This is God's chosen plan for me. It is God's chosen plan for you. As I studied the Gospels, I discovered the qualities of Jesus that challenged my soul as I thought about allowing the Holy Spirit to make me more like Him. While I could write an entire book on the qualities of Jesus we might develop in our lives through reading one gospel account alone, I began to focus on that verse in Ephesians (5:2), which is an invitation to imitate Jesus and live a life of love. Thankfully, Paul explains to us in Romans 12:9–21 what a sacrificial, loving life looks like. He writes, "love must be sincere" (v. 9) and argues that—among many characteristics—sincere love primarily *shows honor to others, contributes to the needs of others, offers hospitality, and associates with people no one else cares about.* Instead of living a self-serving life, chosen people reveal Jesus through lives that love as only He can love. This means that, by faith and through the power of the Holy Spirit, we love with God's love as we go about our ordinary days.

But how does God love? What is Jesus *actually like* as He moves about His earthly life?

If we organize all we might find in the Gospels about Jesus, we could compile three categories that help us think better about Jesus living His resurrected life through us. We can showcase His character and behavior in three ways:

Jesus serves.
Jesus suffers.
Jesus seeks and saves the lost.

JESUS SERVES

We are most like Jesus when the Holy Spirit leads us to bless others as a servant. We continue to shape our lives—in home, work, and ministry—to Philippians 2:1–18.

Let's examine this first category of Christ as a servant through this passage. Paul writes that if we are to stay like-minded with Christ, we are to "do nothing out of selfish ambition or vain conceit." We are to instead "value others above [ourselves], not looking to [our] own interests but . . . to the interests of the others" (vv. 3b–4). What would it look like to live a life where I always consider the interests and well-being of other people because I value their lives above my own? What would it look like to turn from selfish ambition—putting myself first with my goals, desires, and plans—and put others first? Could I live my life in order to make others succeed?

Imagine waking up tomorrow and saying this to your family members: "I would like to make your dreams come true today. I would love to bless you and make your life easier. How can I help you? How can I bless you?"

Now, move into your professional world or community and imagine asking the same question. This isn't as bizarre as you think for Christ followers because Paul continues to explain this new life like this in Philippians 2:5–7a: "In your relationships with one another, have the same mindset as Christ Jesus: Who, being in very nature God, did not consider equality with God something to be used to his own advantage; rather, he made himself nothing by taking the very nature of a servant." Living as "a servant" who makes herself "nothing" presents a model of living far different from the personal mission statements of so many of us who desire high positions of honor and prestige where others serve us.

As I studied the gospel to learn more about *how* Jesus serves, *whom* He serves, *when*, and *where*, I loved observing how Jesus depends upon God's power and direction. He says in John 5:19, "The Son can do nothing by himself; he can do only what he sees his Father doing, because whatever the Father does the Son also does."

Jesus also claims in John 12:49–50, "the Father who sent me commanded me to say all that I have spoken. . . . whatever I say is just what the Father has told me to say."

Later, Jesus explains in John 14:10 that it is the "Father, living in [him], who is doing his work." And finally, Jesus says, "I love the Father and do exactly what my Father has commanded me" (John 14:31). Jesus, in other words, models a dependence on and obedience to God in order to do any service to God. He always points to the Father—not seeking glory for Himself as the Son.

> SOME CHRISTIAN TEACHING TELLS YOU TO KEEP WORKING AND ONE DAY, YOU MIGHT PERFECT YOURSELF ENOUGH THAT YOU'LL BE LIKE HIM. WE THINK THAT PERHAPS WE'LL ONE DAY BE GOOD ENOUGH TO NO LONGER NEED GRACE, FORGIVENESS, AND DAILY POWER TO LIVE THE IMPOSSIBLE CHRISTIAN LIFE.

This matters deeply because some Christian teaching tells you to try harder to be like Jesus. It tells you to keep working and one day you might perfect yourself enough that you'll be like Him. We think that perhaps we'll one day be good enough to no longer need grace, forgiveness, and daily power to live the impossible Christian life. Remember this: we can do nothing by ourselves. Jesus tells us in John

15:5 that apart from Him, we "can do nothing." Observing Jesus' dependence on His Father's direction, power, and wisdom offers us a way to think about becoming like Him in our dependence on the Holy Spirit for everything we do.

The Holy Spirit pays no attention to social conventions (Jesus met with those nobody else would), limited resources (Jesus served five thousand people with five small barley loaves and two small fish in John 6), or concerns for platform and worldly influence (Jesus moved away from crowds and often instructed others to keep quiet about Him as noted in Mark 7:36 and 9:9). Our desire should be for serving others today without any regard for who they are, what we lack, and without anyone announcing our service in church or on social media.

I know I'm chosen for Christ—for His purposes and for Him to live His resurrected life through me. So I ask myself: What would Jesus do if He had my day to live? What would He do with my time, my resources, and my personality? With whom would He spend time?

I think about Jesus inside my home and inside my schedule, and I realize this: Everywhere Jesus went, *He followed God's instructions* in obedience.

His time was not His own; it belonged to the Father.

His reputation was not His own; He entrusted this to the Father.

His comfort was not His own; He endured suffering without retaliating.

Growing as a Christian to become more like Jesus means increasingly dying to self and living for Him. Paul describes this chosen life as being "buried with him through baptism into death in order that, just as Christ was raised from the dead through the glory of the Father, we too may live a new life" (Rom. 6:4). He reminds us "our old self was crucified with him" (v. 6).

This is a crazy, unpredictable, unimaginable life you're about to start living when you tell Jesus you want to be more like Him today. He's going to change your heart, as He is changing mine, and give you the supernatural ability to love new categories of people that Jesus always extends Himself to: brokenhearted people, people you feel are your enemies and undeserving, and, as I shared before, children.

Once I settled the issue that my life was not my own and fully allowed the Holy Spirit to control, direct, and empower my day to make me more like Jesus, supernatural things began happening involving the *brokenhearted, undeserving enemies, and children.* And this isn't a mistake. You're chosen for Christ to become more like Him in His love for people, especially people you find difficult or inconvenient to love. But the whole time, you'll be with Jesus as you love people, and your life will explode with joy and purpose.

Several years ago I marveled over Psalm 34:18 (ESV): "The LORD is near to the brokenhearted and saves the crushed in spirit." I thought about staying "near" to Jesus by somehow drawing near to hurting people—because He is near to them. I wrote this in my journal: *Go find brokenhearted people. You will find Jesus there.* I thought about the grieving, the impoverished, and the sick in my community. *How can I move toward hurting people? What would You have me do, Jesus? Show me where hurting people are or bring them to me. I'm here, and I want to be like You to them.*

I HEARD A KNOCK AT MY DOOR. I IGNORED IT BECAUSE I WAS TOO BUSY PRAYING ABOUT FINDING BROKENHEARTED PEOPLE.

As I wrote the words, I heard a knock at my door. I ignored it because I was too busy praying about finding brokenhearted people.

The knocking continued.

Finally, I answered the door to find a neighbor in distress who needed me to help her with a private, painful matter. As I spent the afternoon with her, I realized God's immediate answer to prayer. I couldn't wait to return home to write the story of that knock on the door.

The next morning I sat down to write, and my phone rang. I ignored it because I was too busy writing about how God brought a brokenhearted person into my life. When the phone kept ringing, I answered it. A woman in unimaginable emotional pain needed help. I left my writing desk and drove to her house.

I knew it honored God to care for the brokenhearted, and He responded to my prayer to minister to them. Along the way, I learned how to give encouragement through the Scriptures, to help women worship God, to teach them to live like treasured possessions, and to belong to this new family of God.

When I finally sat down to write my thoughts, I wrote, *I'm learning I am most like Jesus when I'm serving in the power of the Holy Spirit to brokenhearted people.*

—⚬⚬⚬—

When I'm confused about God's plan for my life or unsure what to do with my day, I remember the invitation to live like Jesus as I care for the brokenhearted and children. But I also know that Jesus offers counterculture wisdom in how we care for those whom we perceive as enemies and those undeserving of our love because of how they have hurt us or damaged our reputations.

Jesus teaches in Matthew 5:44, "Love your enemies and pray for those who persecute you," just as we see Jesus asking God to forgive the very enemies who crucified Him on the cross. In Luke 6:27, 35–36, Jesus further commands,

> But to you who are listening I say: Love your enemies, do good to those who hate you, bless those who curse you, pray for those who mistreat you. . . . love your enemies, do good to them, and lend to them without expecting to get anything back. Then your reward will be great, and you will be children of the Most High, because he is kind to the ungrateful and wicked. Be merciful, just as your Father is merciful.

When you read this passage, do you feel frustrated, angry, convicted, or ashamed? Do you feel, like I do, so far from being a woman who represents the attitude and behavior Jesus commands? I know this: Jesus never makes a command that He doesn't also give us the power to obey. With His power working within us to make us like Jesus, we can approach enemies—those who hate us, who curse us, who mistreat us, who cannot repay us—and we might offer a kind act, a blessing, and a prayer.

A kindness. A blessing. A prayer.

———ᗡᗡ———

I hear my daughter say, "I cannot believe this!" from her bedroom where she's working on rather difficult science homework. "Mom!" she calls out. I find her staring at her phone, mouth open in disbelief. She tells me how a girl who ignores her, who excludes her, and who makes mean comments to her has texted her because she needs help with her science homework. I stand in the doorway with my arms folded, waiting.

"I wonder why she texted you," was my comment. I can see the struggle in my daughter's eyes as anger begins that slow turn to compassion. We had talked about blessing our enemies, about returning meanness with kindness, but I never imagined God would put these principles to the test so quickly.

I return to the kitchen to see what my daughter will do on her own. A few hours later, she says this: "I remembered about being kind to enemies, Mom. So I helped her. I didn't want to do it, but I did. It was the right thing to do."

Perhaps we are most like Jesus when we approach the "ungrateful and wicked" or any perceived enemies through the eyes of compassion. We see Jesus looking out over the crowds of people, and He describes them as "harassed and helpless, like sheep without a shepherd," and "he had compassion on them" (Matt. 9:36). I wonder if, at this moment, the disciples knew that Jesus was the incarnate God, the one proclaimed in Exodus as "the compassionate and gracious God, slow to anger, abounding in love and faithfulness" (34:6). He is David's God of "great compassion" in Psalm 51; He is the priest's God of compassion in Psalm 119; He is Isaiah's God who "will rise up to show [us] compassion" (Isa. 30:18); He is the God of never-failing compassion described by Jeremiah in Lamentations, by Hosea, Joel, Micah, and Zechariah. This compassion moves God to action as Healer, Savior, and Comforter.

When we see the compassion of Jesus that points to the compassion of the Father, let's pray that the Holy Spirit produces the character of Jesus within us as the *compassionate comforter* whom Paul describes as "the God of all comfort" (2 Cor. 1:3)—not only to those who deserve it, but also to those who act as enemies.

Paul tells us about our chosen identity as compassionate comforters, like Jesus, in Colossians 3:12. He says, "Therefore, as God's chosen people, holy and dearly loved, clothe yourselves with compassion, kindness, humility, gentleness and patience." Can you imagine interacting with people in your life—parents, siblings, spouses, children, neighbors, coworkers, even strangers and enemies—as a compassionate comforter? As someone chosen for Christ to reveal the Son to a hurting world?

Chosen men and women live as agents of God's compassionate comfort. We respond with compassion, not only to the brokenhearted and to children in need but also to those who harm us. We seek to do good, to bless, and to pray. When we do these things, we reveal Christ in powerful ways to a world that desperately needs His presence.

JESUS SUFFERS

Jesus serves, yes, but Jesus also suffers. Chosen people become like Jesus in their expectation of, and attitudes toward, suffering.

Jesus *willingly suffers* for others; He lays down His very life. In 1 John 3:16 John writes that "Jesus Christ laid down his life for us. And we ought to lay down our lives for our brothers and sisters." The expected suffering of chosen men and women isn't simply that we serve others in ways that feel like suffering; Scripture teaches that we will suffer as we *turn from sinful desires*, as we *endure any insult or persecution as Christians*, and as we *grow our character through trials* God ordains for us.

Chosen people don't fear suffering or dread it. They *understand* it. They welcome suffering as evidence of God's work to form Christ within them. They interpret suffering through the lens of being chosen.

After describing our chosen identity in the first chapter, Peter tells us this:

> Therefore, since Christ suffered in his body, arm yourselves also with the same attitude, because whoever suffers in the body is done with sin. As a result, they do not live the rest of their earthly lives for evil human desires, but rather for the will of God. (1 Peter 4:1–2)

Being conformed to the image of Christ requires what Scripture calls the "refiner's fire" (Mal. 3:2) and having God "thoroughly purge away your dross" (Isa. 1:25). God works in you what is pleasing to Him. He's actively removing impurities and things in your life that don't please Him. While this process often feels like a death to self and a sacrificing of desire, it's the most important thing happening to you other than the day you received Christ as His chosen child.

Besides people receiving salvation, I can think of nothing more exciting happening anywhere in the world, in any person, than this beautiful truth: Chosen people are becoming more like Jesus. We are, like Peter writes, able to "participate in the divine nature" (2 Peter 1:4). The Holy Spirit invades your life and necessarily disrupts everything in it that hinders you from the chosen life God intends for you.

My own refiner's fire involved the cutting away of everything in my life that didn't help me love God or love others more. In your own life, this "purging of dross" might include the ending of certain relationships, the transformation of lifestyle choices that keep you addicted and less than the person God's shaping, or even the death of the vision you once had for your life as becoming famous or caught up in pleasure you don't think you can live without.

The second predictable and welcomed form of suffering includes the insult or persecution we endure because we follow Jesus. Jesus tells us that those who suffer like this are "blessed" (Matt. 5:10). We also learn in Philippians 1:29 that "it has been granted to you on behalf of Christ not only to believe in him, but also to suffer for him."

What form will this suffering take? What persecution might you welcome for being a Christian? It might include social rejection—like friends who turn from you because of your convictions— or legal persecution like punishment or imprisonment. When we understand that God chooses us to suffer for Him, we remember this is part of our becoming like Christ. Peter tells us to "rejoice inasmuch as you participate in the sufferings of Christ" (1 Peter 4:13).

My daughter was in tears because some girls said she was "too religious" and didn't like how she avoided gossip, wanted to follow the rules, and desired to reach out to those who were unpopular. My neighbor, a wise and godly woman, walked across the street as I called her for help consoling my daughter. She said to my daughter, "I'm so proud of you. The Bible says that when you suffer for doing good, you are blessed." She quoted from 1 Peter 4:14 and 16: "If you are insulted because of the name of Christ, you are blessed, for the Spirit of glory and of God rests on you. . . . if you suffer as a Christian, do not be ashamed, but praise God that you bear that name." We stood on my back porch together as my daughter's tears of sorrow turned to tears of joy: she was God's chosen daughter, and God's favor rested on her in her suffering.

The final category of suffering relates to God's use of trials to form our character. Consider the words from James 1:2–4:

> Consider it pure joy, my brothers and sisters, whenever you face trials of many kinds, because you know that the testing

of your faith produces perseverance. Let perseverance finish its work so that you may be mature and complete, not lacking anything.

Here, we know that God might choose us for a particular trial to build our faith, grow perseverance, and foster the kind of maturity that makes us "complete, not lacking anything." Just as Jesus "learned obedience from what he suffered" (Heb. 5:8), we think about difficult circumstances growing our faith and producing Christlikeness within us.

JESUS SEEKS AND SAVES THE LOST

Jesus serves. Jesus suffers, and finally, Jesus *seeks and saves the lost.*

We become like Jesus as we serve in humility—especially those we find difficult—as we patiently endure suffering with joy, and as we now do what Jesus came to do: seek and save the lost (Luke 19:10).

As someone who loves evangelism and wakes up with expectancy about how God will use me for His kingdom in the lives of others, I didn't expect God to correct something about my personal mission to seek and save the lost in my neighborhood. On many occasions I felt prompted by God to walk around my neighborhood to see if any neighbors just happened to be outside and in need. Twice I discovered neighbors in distress who were crying on the sidewalk. Both times I told these people without any hesitation that *Jesus sent me to find you.* Both times I shared the gospel with these women. My task felt clear, supernatural, and joyful.

But one cold winter morning I felt the same prompting by the Holy Spirit to find hurting neighbors. I stood on my front porch, crossing my arms against the cold weather, and I looked up and down the streets. I said to Jesus, "Look, there's nobody out here.

No hurting person in sight. I'll try again later." I went back into my warm, comfortable house, and immediately I remembered the Bible verse from Luke 19:10: "the Son of Man came to *seek* and to save the lost" (emphasis mine).

I had no problem telling people about Jesus when they happened to cross my path or if it wasn't inconvenient for me, but Jesus didn't just stand on a porch to see if anyone happened to wander by; He went out to *seek* lost people.

And if you know anything about the game of hide-and-seek, the one seeking must look for hidden people. They aren't hanging out in plain view.

I bundled up in my coat, kicked off my fuzzy grey slippers, and found my boots. I left my house and *went seeking*. I felt a little crazy, but I approached the home of a woman I had heard was struggling.

I knocked on the door. She wasn't going to come to me; I needed to be like Jesus and *seek for her*. She answered, and I went in to comfort her, to talk about Jesus, and to embody the compassionate comfort of Jesus. I talked to her about her need for Jesus and that He was our only hope in her hopeless situation.

I'm most like Jesus when I'm *seeking*.

—⟋⟍—

On this new day, you become a seeker of lost people. You become more patient and joyful in trial, and you also welcome an insult because you follow Christ. Chosen people know that the Holy Spirit is at work this very moment to produce the life of Christ within you.

In a sermon delivered in 1855 by Charles Spurgeon titled "Christ's People: Imitators of Him," we read a fine summary of what it means to become more like Jesus. Spurgeon discusses the work of the Holy Spirit to produce Christlikeness in us that evidences itself in four major ways: boldness of action, lovingkindness, humility, and holiness. Rather than working harder to model one's life after Jesus, we abide with Him and become more and more like Him. As Spurgeon's congregants sought to become like Jesus, Spurgeon offered the "best advice [he could] give" to do so. He writes, "seek more of the Spirit of God; for this is the way to become Christ-like."[5]

Chosen people seek more of the Spirit of God. And how do we do this? Well, something else to notice about Jesus—something a seminary professor mentioned as well—is how much Jesus loves and uses God's Word. This professor suggested that Deuteronomy was Jesus' favorite book of the Bible because He quoted it so much. I checked for myself, and it's true: Jesus uses words from Deuteronomy most of all, especially to defeat Satan in the temptation in the wilderness. When I think about becoming more like Christ, I think about becoming a lover of God's Word to know the voice of the Holy Spirit.

As we study the Word of God to allow the Holy Spirit to transform us more and more to be like Jesus, we remember how He serves (empowered by God), whom He serves (children, the brokenhearted, our enemies), and His embracing of suffering. We also see how, most of all, Jesus came to seek and save the lost. We are most like Him when we serve, suffer, and seek like this. Chosen people, then, adopt a new viewpoint on their ordinary day. They see their circumstances as helping to conform them to the image of Christ. They are chosen for this marvelous work, perhaps the most exciting thing happening in the world today.

We are becoming like the Son.

YOUR NEXT STEP

Read one of the gospel accounts (Matthew, Mark, Luke, or John), and make note of every time you see Jesus' speech and behavior. What patterns do you notice?

1. What would Jesus do if He had your time and your schedule today?

2. When you think of the categories of Christlikeness as serving, suffering, and seeking the lost, talk about how you already see God forming Christ in you in this way.

3. Where in your life can you move toward those difficult for you to love, toward brokenhearted people, or toward those you perceive as enemies? How could you serve them?

4. What mindset enables a Christian to "consider it pure joy" when they face trials?

CHAPTER 11

THE SEVENTH INVITATION: LIVE DIFFERENTLY FROM THE WORLD

Do not conform to the pattern of this world,
but be transformed by the renewing of your mind.

—ROMANS 12:2

The world is no longer the natural habitat
for men who have been born again.

—PASTOR AND AUTHOR MARK BUBECK

You probably feel like a froglet right now.

If you've stepped into a new life by living chosen to worship, to live as a treasured possession, to belong to a new family, to complete good works, to display God's power, to become like Jesus, you might already feel that you're living a life profoundly different from the rest of the world. Plus, you're looking forward to an eternity with Jesus as His chosen one, and life's feeling more spiritual than material. You feel like you're not in your natural habitat anymore. You nod your head when you read one theologian say, "We act awkward here because we belong up there."[1]

That "awkward" feeling—or the feeling that this isn't quite home—reminds me of the froglet. When you aren't a tadpole in the water anymore, but you still aren't fully a land frog, you're a *froglet*. On the way to becoming a frog, the tadpole endures a curious in-between stage that biologists call *the froglet phase*.

She has lungs but finds herself strangely still in water. She has feet but can't yet manage the land. Now a foreigner in the place she once believed her home, she cannot even breathe. Her gills betray her, and her tail that helps her swim disappears. All the things that once worked to bring her life now fail her.

I relate. Can you?

In John 15:19 Jesus tells us something about our chosen lives. He says, "The world would love you as one of its own if you belonged to it, but you are no longer part of the world. I chose you to come out of the world. . ." (NLT).

God chooses us to come "out of the world." A froglet doesn't quite fit in her environment because she's made for a different one. God has transformed us, and now we need to know how to live here.

I remember seeing those froglets in the creek back in Virginia as they fan a worthless stub of tail, unable to take in life from their environment. But if you watch them, they know exactly what to do: they burst through the water's surface to gulp that breath of air.

Something about coming to the surface like that resonates deeply. We live like froglets, no longer fit for this habitat, gulping for spiritual truth, for spiritual refreshment, because that's now our only possible satisfaction. When the frantic froglet realizes her gills and tail won't work—and they shouldn't because she's being transformed into a new creation—she propels herself up and out of that dark underwater world and up into the light. There's a whole world outside of the darkness. We now live in the light and breathe deeply of the Holy Spirit. Soon, we'll look around.

There's glorious land ahead, and you're about to live differently from all the ways you knew before.

———⟋⟋⟍———

When I was twenty-one years old I memorized Psalm 16. I recited it as I walked around the campus of the University of Michigan. When I felt suffocated by a world demanding I work for recognition, fame, and wealth, Psalm 16 became my oxygen to refresh my toxic lungs. This psalm showed me a way to live differently from the rest of the world. David writes:

Keep me safe, my God,
    for in you I take refuge.

I say to the LORD, "You are my Lord;
    apart from you I have no good thing."
I say of the holy people who are in the land,
    "They are the noble ones in whom is all my delight."
Those who run after other gods will suffer more and more.
    I will not pour out libations of blood to such gods
    or take up their names on my lips.

LORD, you alone are my portion and my cup;
    you make my lot secure.
The boundary lines have fallen for me in pleasant places;
    surely I have a delightful inheritance.
I will praise the LORD, who counsels me;
    even at night my heart instructs me.

I keep my eyes always on the LORD.
  With him at my right hand, I will not be shaken.

Therefore my heart is glad and my tongue rejoices;
  my body also will rest secure,
because you will not abandon me to the realm of the dead,
  nor will you let your faithful one see decay.
You make known to me the path of life;
  you will fill me with joy in your presence,
  with eternal pleasures at your right hand.

This chosen life—lived so differently from the rest of the world—would forever hold the truth that, apart from God, we have "no good thing" (v. 2). It would forever know how our sorrow and suffering increase if we chase after anything other than Him (v. 4). It would be a life of surrender to the life God ordains, knowing that the boundary lines He sets are "pleasant" (v. 6); God secures us, counsels us, and sets us on the path of life (vv. 5, 7, 11); and His presence always fills us with joy (v. 11).

As I meditated on this psalm over the next twenty years, what most captured my attention were the words "path of life." What is this *path of life*? We know that Jesus says He is our "life" and offers an abundant, full life (John 10:10). We know that we "find our life" when we lose it for Jesus (Matt. 10:39). I wanted to forever stay on this "path of life," and I want to choose the right path each new day.

In Deuteronomy 30:19–20, I love how clearly Moses frames the truth. He describes two paths—one of curses and destruction, and one of life and prosperity. He tells the people, "Now choose life, so that you and your children may live and that you may love the LORD your God, listen to his voice, and hold fast to him. For the LORD is your life . . ."

The Lord is my life. Can you say He is your life? We have life in His Son, Jesus. Apart from Him we are dead. And now we walk on the path of life. We daily choose to stay on this path of life. Let us "take hold of the life that is truly life" (1 Tim. 6:19) and not turn aside from this path.

I didn't want to be on the path described in Proverbs 14:12 that seems right but leads to death. I didn't want to be on the dark and slippery path described by Jeremiah (23:12). I wanted to stay on the path of God's commands that the psalmist in Psalm 119 describes as a delight, as peaceful, as straight, and as gleaming with light.

Or, I could travel down the dark, unstable, dangerous paths. I could fall for the traps and snares of the enemy who schemes against us to take us off God's path. In both Psalms 140 and 141 we read of traps and snares along our paths.

But chosen people know the path of life already because of the seven invitations. On this day we consecrate ourselves—knowing we're chosen for Christ and not our own glory—so we step into the path of worship, of living as His treasured possession,

BUT WE MUST STAND AGAINST A CULTURE THAT PRESENTS DARK AND SLIPPERY PATHS. THE GLAMOR OF THESE PATHS MAY APPEAR AS LIGHT, BUT THEY LEAD US TO TREACHEROUS PLACES.

as belonging to a new family, completing good works, of being conformed to His image, and of living differently from the rest of the world.

This is the life we've been missing.

But we must stand against a culture that presents dark and slippery paths. We expose the dark and slippery paths that seduce us with wealth, fame, or self-fulfillment. The glamor of these paths may appear as light—since we know "Satan himself masquerades as an angel of light" (2 Cor. 11:14)—but they lead us to treacherous places.

Following the false light of self-fulfillment—where the goal of our lives is our own satisfaction, personal happiness, and comfort—may seem the right of every individual. But God warns us that, as we pursue riches and pleasures, we are like blooms that become "choked" and never mature (Luke 8:14).

Picture yourself as a lovely flower. Now picture pleasure and riches choking the stem with cruel, unrelenting hands. As we grow greedy for more and more pleasure and wealth, Jesus sternly cries in Luke 12:15, "Watch out! Be on your guard against all kinds of greed; life does not consist in an abundance of possessions." Chosen people know that when they lose their life, they find it. When they stop seeking fulfillment and comfort and keep their eyes fixed on Jesus, all that they need will be provided for them.

The path of life I find most challenging in living differently from the rest of the world includes the path of *living a humble life of service in a culture of self-exaltation.* I think about how John the Baptist said that he must become *less* and Jesus become *more* as he advanced into his life (John 3:30).

I often think about the life of Dr. Bill Bright when I consider someone who lived differently from the rest of the world. His life became less; Jesus became more. You might not know who he is. Exactly! Many people did not know when he died on July 19, 2003.

The day passed with relative silence in the news. If you asked someone on the street, they most likely wouldn't know him. But Dr. Bright founded the world's largest missions organization that employs 26,000 staff, involves 225,000 volunteers, and maintains a presence in 191 countries. In 1956 he wrote a little booklet on knowing God personally that went into translation in over 200 languages; the *Four Spiritual Laws* booklet has been distributed to 2.5 billion people as the most disseminated religious booklet in history. Dr. Bright received the Templeton Prize for Progress in Religion and promptly donated the $1 million prize to encourage worldwide prayer and fasting.[2]

I had worked for the ministry of Campus Crusade for Christ International for years, and I didn't know anything about this publishing success, this prize money, or even the fact that at one time, Dr. Bright spoke to a crowd of three million at an evangelism event in South Korea. These represent only a small fraction of Dr. Bright's global influence, but what astonishes me is *how little we talk about him*. We talk about Jesus, not Dr. Bright. We talk about knowing God personally, the Spirit-filled life, and training in evangelism instead. Fame and wealth never mattered to Dr. Bright. He wanted us to quote Jesus, not him.

I think about my life as a college instructor, writer, and speaker. Could I ever live in humble service like Dr. Bright? What does Jesus say about roles of influence in society? In the ancient world the Jewish scribes were teachers of the law who carefully translated, copied, and interpreted manuscripts, much like humanities professors today and Christian speakers and writers. Scribes were educated and devoted their lives to the study of their fields, which in this case was Old Testament writing. Like many Christian expositors, scribes offered authoritative commentary.

Three of the gospel writers—Matthew (an eyewitness and disciple of Jesus), Mark (the traveling companion of Peter), and Luke (the traveling companion of Paul)—record Jesus' clear warning against the attitude and behavior of the scribes. In Matthew 23:5–7, Jesus says the following:

> Everything they do is done for people to see: They make their phylacteries wide and the tassels on their garments long; they love the place of honor at banquets and the most important seats in the synagogues; they love to be greeted with respect in the marketplaces and to be called "Rabbi" by others.

Did you notice the three dangerous behaviors? The scribes love to distinguish themselves by their *outward display of superiority*, their *acknowledgment from others* in the marketplace, and their *honorable seating*. They love status. They love recognition. They love being important. They love people looking at them.

Do these attitudes feel familiar to any of us? If we're being honest with one another, we know that we love feeling important—not just in obvious ways like making a name for ourselves at work but also in subtle ways right down to the clothing we wear for others to notice. Clothing for the scribes (the phylacteries held Scripture in leather boxes and the tassels were to remind them of the law) was simply about being noticed as *superior and holy*. For the scribes Jesus addresses, everything was about being noticed by others. Everything was about the appearance of holiness and being more important than other people.

I think they wanted to feel *chosen*, just like we do.

When I read Jesus' warning about the scribes and hear His rebuke, I immediately feel the conviction of sin that I, too, like to exalt myself. I, too, like to be noticed. I love attention and recognition. I love awards, honors, and special seating. Part of the reason being "chosen" resonated so deeply with me is because I knew I was still waiting to be publicly chosen.

As we study the New Testament, we see that Jesus offers a gospel alternative to self-promotion and self-exaltation: our lives become "crucified with Christ" (Gal. 2:20) and "hidden with Christ" (Col. 3:3). Rather than living a self-important life that is always on display, we are encouraged in the Gospels to do the opposite: we are to do much more "in secret" than in the public arena. Jesus tells us in Matthew 6 that the Lord rewards those who pray, fast, and give "in secret." Indeed, Jesus' admonition is clear: do not perform for public approval, honor, recognition, and attention.

Jesus cared nothing about superiority, recognition, and outward signs of importance.

Jesus knew He was already chosen, seen, loved, and delighted in by the Father.

May we remember that Someone does indeed see us and Someone does choose and acknowledge us. Jesus offers a richer and more satisfying acknowledgment than any academic prize, public announcement, or social media crowd. I've realized that this *greater acknowledgment* makes all other forms of being chosen nearly trivial.

MAY WE REMEMBER THAT SOMEONE DOES INDEED SEE US AND SOMEONE DOES CHOOSE AND ACKNOWLEDGE US. JESUS OFFERS A RICHER AND MORE SATISFYING ACKNOWLEDGMENT THAN ANY ACADEMIC PRIZE, PUBLIC ANNOUNCEMENT, OR SOCIAL MEDIA CROWD.

I have learned to rest in the answer and let myself acknowledge the ache I've always had to feel chosen.

And I know God chooses me.

Just last night I had a special moment of *being less* with Jesus. I made the mistake of scrolling Twitter to take note of what other Christian women writers were talking about. I found the tweet of a woman I once shared a stage with at a speaking event several years ago. At the time she wasn't as well-known as she is today. Now she has thousands of followers and obvious friendships with other famous Christian women who responded to her tweets and posted pictures of themselves with her at some kind of gathering.

I suddenly felt the same ache from middle school that led me to write *Seated with Christ* just a few years ago. There was a popular Christian women writers table, and I'm not invited. Tears formed in my eyes as I looked at the cover of her book that showcased endorsements from all the great Christian women—the same women whose marketing managers and publicists told me that they didn't have time to read my manuscript for an endorsement.

I'll never be that woman. I'll never be that special, followed, or known. I'll never have a seat at their table.

I went to the kitchen to clean up the dinner dishes. I remembered that I was seated at the best table already with Jesus (Eph. 2:6), but I had never felt so invisible, so small in my body. Meekness spread over my heart. A sweet presence seemed to fill my soul. I told Jesus that I was going to live a hidden, small life. I didn't need to exalt myself or show off; I didn't need celebrity friends. I didn't need anything but the acknowledgment of my Savior.

I chose you. I chose you to belong to Me. You are chosen. I see you. I appointed you to bear fruit I designed just for you.

I sensed His pleasure. I heard His voice through the Scriptures I had been reading about being chosen for Him.

⁓⁓

Chosen people live differently from the rest of the world, most notably by their humble, secret service that exalts Jesus and not themselves. But they also live differently because of their pursuit of godliness in speech and action.

The first time I felt different from the rest of the world as a Christian was as a thirteen-year-old. My friends began drinking alcohol and kissing boys, and I learned from my youth group pastor that God wanted something different for Christians. I had read the Bible's words about sexual purity and not becoming drunk, but my friends were moving in that direction. It all looked so fun—just like what all the teen movies of the '80s had promised us: parties and romance. In fact, every one of those John Hughes films taught me that the goal of my teen life was to be *chosen*. Up until that point, I fed my mind with *Pretty in Pink*, *Sixteen Candles*, and *Some Kind of Wonderful*. The whole point was to find love, go to a great party, and walk off into your fabulous chosen life.

I stood in the locker room after changing into my gym clothes, and a former close friend said, "You're just so *good*, aren't you?" She rolled her eyes and huffed away from me, impatient and embarrassed for me for leaving parties and talking about living a pure life.

I knew that living as a Christian wasn't going to be easy or normal. It might mean seasons of loneliness. It might bring social rejection. It would mean writing a new movie script for my life—the one where Jesus chooses me and the life I'm supposed to live in holiness, purity, and purpose. In this script, the chosen one finds indescribable joy, peace, and a love far surpassing Jake Ryan kissing her on top of his living room table (or, to bring the image to modern day, the last kiss in nearly every Hallmark movie).

It was going to take faith to believe this. It was going to take believing that Jesus, and the life He offered, was truly abundant, truly magnificent, and truly worth losing everything for. God was already changing my heart. I felt what Pastor Mark Bubeck promised when he wrote that the Holy Spirit can "put within us greater values and desires than those which the world offers."³

As I read my Bible, prayed, and began to make friends with godly people, I found myself *wanting* to obey in the areas of sexual purity, godly speech, and ridding myself of "everything that contaminates body and spirit, perfecting holiness out of reverence for God" (2 Cor. 7:1). The verb "rid" or "avoid" appears several times in the New Testament as a great place to start living differently from the rest of the world.

> YOU'LL BEGIN TO UNDERSTAND THAT YOU'RE MADE FOR A DIFFERENT HOME WHEN DECIDING THAT WALKING WITH JESUS AS HIS CHOSEN ONE MATTERS MORE THAN ALL THE PLEASURES ON EARTH.

Paul writes, for example, "But now you must also rid yourselves of all such things as these: anger, rage, malice, slander, and filthy language from your lips" (Col. 3:8). He also instructs about sexual purity in 1 Thessalonians 4:3–4 by claiming, "It is God's will that you should be sanctified: that you should avoid sexual immorality; that each of you should learn to control your own body in a way that is holy and honorable."

You'll feel like that froglet when you make choices that honor God in your dating life. But you'll begin to understand that you're made for a different home when deciding that walking with Jesus as His chosen one matters more than all the pleasures on earth.

—⟋⟍—

Now, in my professional life, I know I'm different in many ways—from my love of grammar and vivid verbs to my lack of fashion sense—but lately what people have noticed about me is *joy and thanksgiving* in a culture of complaint and criticism. Jesus has changed my bad attitude to one of rejoicing. Only because of Him have others noticed a radiance of Christ within me that their hearts respond to.

When you live as chosen to live differently from the rest of the world, people will notice.

In Philippians 2:14–16, after Paul talks about living in humility—without any selfish ambition or self-interest—he describes the effect we have on others when we live chosen out of this world to rejoice:

> Do everything without grumbling or arguing, so that you may become blameless and pure, "children of God without fault in a warped and crooked generation." Then you will shine among them like stars in the sky as you hold firmly to the word of life.

What captures my heart in this passage is how chosen children of God will "shine like stars" in the universe. We will shine in dark places. We will shine so others find their way to Jesus. We will shine, not to bring light to our own faces for fame and attention, but so that we illuminate God's Word that we "hold out" in front of us.

Christians do live differently from the rest of the world, and they speak about this kind of living with confidence and joy because they know that God's commands are a pathway to joy and abundant life.

YOUR NEXT STEP

Read Romans 12:1–2.

1. List out examples of what you think the "pattern of the world" is.

2. How do you sense God asking you to live differently from the rest of the world? What attitudes and areas of your life would change?

3. When people encounter Christians, what is the first thing you think people should notice about them?

4. In what ways do you feel like this world is no longer your natural habitat?

PART THREE

WHAT IF I SAY YES?

CHAPTER 12

A DAILY CONSECRATION

*Consecrate yourselves, for tomorrow the
Lord will do amazing things among you.*

—Joshua 3:5

*Do not act, at any time, as if you are not priests. If you profess to
be the Lord's, do not lie about it, let it be truly so—and that every
day, and all the day, and in all things, for He has made us kings.*

—Nineteenth-century preacher
Charles Spurgeon

I'm up early to walk my neighbor's dog, Peanut—a poodle-terrier mix who looks exactly like a peanut—while his humans travel to Philadelphia. The sun rises above the trees, and the morning air arrives fresh and cold on my face. The rhythm of walking feels so peaceful in this quiet neighborhood as families stir from their beds. I think about the chores of the day: laundry, grocery shopping, housecleaning, and writing. After I drop Peanut at home, I'll drink coffee and pray about the day. But first, I'm working out another word in Scripture related to my chosen identity—a word that is so joyfully mixed with holy fear that it feels sublime. It's the word I've ignored up to now: *priesthood*. We are a chosen *priesthood*.

I walk behind Peanut and, for the first time in my life, I proclaim that Jesus chose me to serve as a priest—to minister before Him in holiness and reverence, to pronounce blessing, to announce the way to God through the blood sacrifice of Jesus, and to help others on their spiritual journey.

I feel taller. I tilt my chin up into the cold morning air. Jesus chose me to serve as a priest. Right here in my ordinary world—with Peanut and laundry and groceries—I take on the consecrated role of a priest in a chosen priesthood.

Can this be right? Is this part of my chosen identity? Peter says so in 1 Peter 2:9, but I'm laughing as I crunch over the snow-covered lawn, dragging the part of my shoe that landed in dog poop to clean it as best as I can. *Is this really what a chosen priesthood looks like?*

I kicked off my shoes and entered the warm house where coffee and my Bible awaited, and I scanned the Scriptures. It *is* true: Isaiah tells us that we "will be called priests of the LORD, [we] will be named ministers of our God" (61:6). Indeed, Paul tells us that we are "competent as ministers of a new covenant" (2 Cor. 3:6) under Jesus Christ. In the vision God gives to John in Revelation, we're immediately told this: "To him who loves us and has freed us from our sins by his blood, and has made us to be a kingdom and priests to serve his God and Father—to him be glory and power for ever and ever!" (1:5b–6)

We are chosen priests. I can hardly believe it. Have you ever in your life thought of yourself in this way?

In a sermon delivered November 15, 1874, called "The Consecration of Priests," Charles Spurgeon explains our chosen identity as serving in the office of the spiritual priesthood.[1] He explains that, unlike Old Testament priests chosen by God, we undergo no outward rituals for purification; we wear no outward priestly clothing;

we receive no outward anointing; and we do not participate in preparing the sacrifices.

Now, the requirements of our becoming priests has been completely accomplished by Jesus Christ. He purifies us, clothes us with righteousness, anoints us with His power, and enables us to become living sacrifices. We live every moment with a "clear view of the Lord Jesus as [our] sin offering and substitute."[2] And, like the priest who stood with hands full of the burnt animal and the bread offered, we stand with full hands to feed the people around us with God's Word.

Spurgeon writes, "When the Lord ordains His people to be priests unto Him, He puts the Bible into their hands, and fills their heads and hearts with the truth of God. When you have the inspired Word in your hands . . . you have all sorts of spiritual food for all sorts of persons."[3] Further, whatever fullness in our hands God gives us—financial resources, spiritual gifts, natural talents, time, possessions—we consecrate these things to God. This "fullness is meant for the distribution to God's glory."[4]

What more do priests do? How do they behave? I thought of the priests in the Old Testament chosen to carry the ark of the covenant, chosen to enter the holy of holies, and chosen to purify locations. I thought of how the priests chosen by God were to have no inheritance of land because the Lord Himself was their special inheritance. They belonged to God, and they physically carried objects of His power and blessing. How do we do this as a part of a New Testament priesthood? How do we see ourselves carrying all of these things in our soul to somehow distribute to people wherever we go?

What a calling! What a divine privilege to see ourselves as a holy agent of God's power and blessing and as the one leading others into Christ's atoning work on their behalf.

With this realization, I move into my day with purpose and power, a rescuer of souls that belong to Christ. I can think of no better picture of what I'm doing as part of a chosen priesthood than a scene in a movie that brings me to tears with its power and beauty. In *The Lord of the Rings: The Fellowship of the Rings*, terrible forces of evil, the Black Riders, come after Frodo Baggins, who now nears death. Arwen, a Half-elven beautiful and noble maiden, singlehandedly rescues Frodo by calling forth a flood and wielding her sword. But Frodo still nearly dies. Arwen takes the weak Frodo into her arms and cries, "No, Frodo, no! Don't give in. Not now." And then she prays, "What grace is given me, let it pass to him. Let him be spared. Save him."[5]

> CHOSEN PEOPLE STEP FORWARD. IMAGINE THIS SPOKEN OVER YOUR LIFE: "STEP FORWARD! THE LORD HAS CHOSEN YOU TO MINISTER AND PRONOUNCE BLESSINGS IN THE NAME OF THE LORD!"

As the music swells, I find myself in tears. I see myself as God's chosen one to find people pursued by darkness, nearing death, hopeless and afraid. I want to take them into my arms like Arwen and beg for God's mercy and healing in their lives. I want to live as the chosen priests who, we're told in Deuteronomy 21:5, "step forward, for the LORD your God has chosen them to minister and to pronounce blessings in the name of the LORD."

Chosen people step forward.

Imagine this spoken over your life: "Step forward! The Lord has chosen you to minister and pronounce blessings in the name of the Lord!"

Step forward.

As part of the chosen priesthood, I cannot escape the need for consecration. The priests were consecrated—set apart, holy, purified, special. To consecrate means to *declare and set apart as sacred.* Do you remember the image of me with my rear end in the air as I fell over like a beached whale at the platform? In that moment, I fell down before the Lord to consecrate myself. I asked Jesus to take me once again as a living sacrifice. I thought of 2 Corinthians 7:1 as I prayed. Paul commands this: "let us purify ourselves from everything that contaminates body and spirit, perfecting holiness out of reverence for God."

Even though I know I have been already declared righteous before God because of Jesus Christ and I live without condemnation (Rom. 8:1), I still take seriously the effect of sin in my life and my need for regular confession and repentance. First John 1:9 states our path to staying purified before the Lord. We read, "If we confess our sins, he is faithful and just and will forgive us our sins and purify us from all unrighteousness."

What contaminates our body? What contaminates our soul? What have we allowed into our lives that distracts us from *wholehearted devotion to Jesus?* What activities in our lives help us love God and love others more, and which activities might we confess, repent of, and prune away?

Chosen men and chosen women decontaminate their lives. They ask the Holy Spirit to regularly point out sin. They live lives of regular confession and repentance to turn from sin. They dedicate every area of their lives to Jesus to be used for His purposes.

They live chosen days—sacred, special, consecrated days.

I live in the necessity of daily consecration; I cannot begin a new day without mentally giving myself afresh entirely to Jesus for His purposes. I do this because it doesn't take very long for me to fall back into old patterns of thinking. It doesn't take very long to become a false self, a flesh-driven diva, and a frantic woman desperately searching for happiness everywhere but in Jesus.

Tomorrow, I'll consecrate myself again. I thought of the words of South African preacher Andrew Murray who summarized the journey God had taken me on. He writes,

"To attain the life of permanent and perfect abiding is not ordinarily given at once as a possession for the future: it comes mostly step by step. Avail yourself, therefore, of every opportunity of exercising the trust of the present moment."[6]

Each new day I set myself apart for Jesus. I inhabit the chosen identity of consecrated priest. I bring the blessing of Jesus and the words of eternal life as I talk about this chosen life in Christ.

YOUR NEXT STEP

Read 1 Peter 2:4–11.

1. What image comes to your mind when you think of yourself as a "royal priest"?

2. If you saw your ordinary day as sacred and consecrated to the Lord, how would this change your attitude and daily experience?

3. If you could "pronounce blessings" on people in your life today, what would you say in your blessing over them?

4. Make a list of ways you wish to "decontaminate your life."

CHAPTER 13

—ᘯᘯ—

A NEW CALLING
AND PURPOSE

As it is, He has led me on, step by step, answering my prayers in His own way; and I cannot bear to have a single human being doubt that it has been a perfect way. I love and adore it just as it is.

—ELIZABETH PAYSON PRENTISS, RECORDED IN 1869
IN HER JOURNAL

W hen I first considered myself a disciple of Christ—a true follower, a surrendered soul—I imagined Jesus first as coming alongside me in the life I was already living. In this scenario, Jesus came to fulfill my dreams of becoming a literature professor who would live in a beautiful home filled with fine art and expensive furniture. I would marry a poet perhaps, or a musician, and Jesus would always be there to help me when I needed Him.

As I began to study my Bible and collect a library of wisdom from Christian missionaries, devotional writers, and theologians, I realized that my notion of Jesus as my partner in aiding the realization of life dreams wasn't just *totally wrong*, it was also ridiculous and so self-centered I'm ashamed to admit it. I began the process of concluding what Elizabeth Prentiss concludes after a lifetime of following Jesus. She writes in her journal on May 26, 1846: "This is the testimony of all the good books, sermons, hymns, and memoirs I read—that God's ways are infinitely perfect; that we are to love Him for what He is and therefore equally as much when He afflicts as when He prospers us; that there is no real happiness but in doing and suffering His will."[1]

Would I do His will? Would I do whatever it took to follow Jesus?

———※———

I sat in Einstein's Bagels in Ann Arbor, Michigan, during the second year of my PhD program. My future husband, Ashley, had asked me on a date for coffee and bagels. We began to have the strangest conversation, a conversation that would change both our lives. Ashley wanted to tell me that he returned from walking in Ann Arbor's famous cemetery. He talked about walking by all those people in their graves in that shady cemetery, going on and on and on about dead people.

I'm thinking: *This is not a romantic date. This is creepy.*

Ashley leaned over the table and said, "I read all those gravestones." He continued, "And I wondered what made their lives significant. Look at us! What are we working so hard for?" He was going to be the world's leading research chemist. Maybe he would win a Nobel Prize. I would write an award-winning dissertation and land a tenure track job, maybe at an Ivy League school.

Ashley put down his bagel and asked, "Why does God leave us here on earth? Why are we here? Why are we *still here*? He could immediately take us to heaven to be with Him. He could sanctify us immediately! So why are we here?"

I had wondered the same thing the summer before when a

Christian friend asked me if I knew what the purpose of my life was. I had said this:

"To be a professor."

She said, "That's not what I mean. That's your job. What's your *purpose?*"

I stared at her with anger bubbling up in my heart. Wasn't serving as a professor good enough for her? Wasn't it prestigious and important? Wasn't it a noble plan? I answered, "Well, I guess to be a *Christian* professor, I need to follow Jesus as a Christian professor." I thought that would silence her and we could move on in our conversation. I thought I had provided the right and biblical answer.

She looked at me and said the words I will never forget.

"Following Jesus means making disciples."

I stopped listening to her. I knew she would quote Jesus' words about sending us out into the world to preach the gospel and make disciples. But that was for missionaries, not me. God hadn't chosen me to become a missionary.

But her words stuck with me.

Two months later—and a few days before meeting Ashley in the bagel shop—I found myself in a campus Bible study where a woman introduced me to a book by Walter Henrichsen on being a disciple of Christ called *Disciples Are Made Not Born*. In a chapter called "The Type of Person God Uses," Henrichsen argues that someone surrendered to Jesus Christ will "[adopt] the same objective in life that God sets forth in the Scriptures."[2] I underlined the sentence and furrowed my eyebrows. I chewed one nail down to nubbins. I kept reading with both fear and joy: joy because I felt the nudging of the Holy Spirit, but fear because I knew that God was about to change something in me forever.

Henrichsen wrote, "Whatever your vocation is, it must never be your life objective; for your vocation, no matter how noble it may be, is, in the final analysis, temporal. The Scriptures teach us that we are to give our lives to the eternal and not to the temporal. A faithful man is a man who has chosen eternal objectives for his life."[3]

Now over coffee and bagels I looked at Ashley and waited. How could I put into words what I had been feeling? How could I explain what God was stirring up in me? Before I could speak, Ashley said, "We are here to participate with Jesus in the greatest thing happening in the world—that people are dead in their sins and Jesus is making them alive in Christ—He is catching people—and we can cooperate with Jesus to bring in this great harvest of people."

He is catching *people*. I saw Peter and his nets. I saw the miraculous catch of fish. Years later I would hear a professor speculate that Jesus filled Peter's nets with what was most likely 3,000 fish—the amount it would take to break the nets. I remember how Peter stood up in Acts 2 and delivered a message of salvation. He caught 3,000 *people* that day—the same "catch" Jesus modeled on the Sea of Galilee. I'm not sure anyone can know how many fish it took to break the nets—and I'm terrible with both math and physics—but the idea that God would bring in a miraculous catch of people to mirror the miraculous catch of fish delights my soul.

I swallowed my coffee in a big gulp. I knew what was happening. That day Ashley and I began to leave our nets to follow Jesus into a new chosen calling. We were chosen for Him and appointed to bear fruit for eternal, kingdom purposes. I still worked hard at my career: I did finish my PhD. I did win awards. I did publish. I did get to teach at the college level. But I lived for a Person, not a plan. It was for His people, not my plan. God would use those career paths to connect me in divine ways to bless people and announce to them the good news that a Savior has come to forgive their sin and welcome them into His kingdom.

If I could tell my own daughters one thing about their time here on earth, I would tell them that they are still here on earth because God has them on a rescue mission for people. Along the way they live a life of worship, of experiencing life as a treasured possession, of belonging to a new family, of becoming more like Jesus, of bearing the fruit of godly character and new converts, of displaying His power, and of living differently from the rest of the world.

But the *plan* for their lives? I'm not sure, and it doesn't essentially matter anymore. God chose them for a Person, not a plan. The plan will surely arrive as they use their spiritual gifts, hone their natural talents, and follow their desires to bless the world through any kind of work they choose. But the plan rests under the purpose: to live as chosen people on a mission to rescue people alongside Jesus. And part of this work isn't as difficult as you'd think. Paul explains our training for it in 2 Timothy 2:2: "And the things you have heard me say in the presence of many witnesses entrust to reliable people who will also be qualified to teach others."

Whatever God was teaching me—beginning in that bagel shop in Ann Arbor—I would pass on to others—through writing, through speaking, through acts of service. I knew He chose me for this.

And you? What has God taught you that He intends for you to pass on?

How is God stirring in you a commitment to eternal things?

—⟨⟩—

I pray for my family and myself the same prayer Paul prays for the Colossians in 1:9–14. In this prayer you'll find the seven invitations that Scripture, in its entirety, lays out for chosen people. And in this prayer, you'll find a wonderful example of a life purpose. Paul writes,

> For this reason, since the day we heard about you, we have not stopped praying for you. We continually ask God to fill you with the knowledge of his will through all the wisdom and understanding that the Spirit gives, so that you may live a life worthy of the Lord and please him in every way: bearing fruit in every good work, growing in the knowledge of God, being strengthened with all power according to his glorious might so that you may have great endurance and patience, and giving joyful thanks to the Father, who has qualified you to share in the inheritance of his holy people in the kingdom of light. For he has rescued us from the dominion of darkness and brought us into the kingdom of the Son he loves, in whom we have redemption, the forgiveness of sins.

Did you see what a chosen life looks like? It bears fruit, grows in the knowledge of God, displays power, responds in worship and thanksgiving, rejoices in a new, holy family, lives in light and not darkness, and lives in light of redemption and forgiveness of sins in a new kingdom. I think of myself as the treasured possession of God, chosen for Christ, to step into this new way of living.

How about you?

Knowing you are chosen for Christ, you now approach the day with seven key questions that change everything about how you experience life. Ask yourself:

1. How will I enter into worship here by increasing my awareness of God's presence, His good character, and His excellence, especially in light of daily provision, providential care, and His eternal perspective?

2. Where do I see evidence of God treating me as His treasured possession—either through physical demonstrations or through the internal comfort, love, and joy from the Holy Spirit?

3. As a person chosen to belong to and serve the family of God, how can I bless people in my life today with the care of a *parent*, the encouragement and camaraderie of a *sibling*, or the joyful playfulness and dependence of a *child*?

4. Who in my life doesn't know Jesus yet, and who needs a blessing?

5. What prayer requests can I lay before the Lord to wait in expectation of His display of power on my behalf?

6. How can I respond to this day as Jesus would—being conformed to His image—as I care for children, the brokenhearted, and even my enemies?

7. How will I live differently from the rest of the world today?

—⟦⟧—

It's snowing again in Pennsylvania. I'm driving downtown with the trees and mountains on my left. I had just spent time with my friend—the neighbor who, out of a Hindu background, prayed to receive Christ because as I kept talking about Jesus she said she wanted to hear everything I had to say about Him—and I decide to stop at a new thrift store.

I'm looking for a spring jacket to wear for a speaking event in April. Lately, I'm speaking more and more about evangelism, and I smile thinking about God bringing people to me who need to know Him. *Who's next, God? Who will it be today?*

As I pull into the thrift store parking lot, I realize it's so small it only has six spots for cars to park. I wish our town had a glamorous mall, and I wish I had the money to afford Nordstrom's or Bloomingdale's. In this fantasy, I would purchase expensive face serums like Estée Lauder's Advanced Night Repair and buy the largest bottle of fancy perfume. But that isn't my life. God didn't choose me for that kind of life.

He chose me for *this* life. I know I'm chosen. And lately, of all the reasons God chose me, I love that I'm His treasured possession most of all. I think about Kate's Day of Chocolate. I think about God answering Sarah with shrimp and grits and text messages from friends. I'm thinking about how Jesus loves His children *so much* and how He actively displays His love to them.

I walk into the thrift store, and the little bell on the door rings out. The owner greets me. *Does she need to know You, Jesus? Lead me, and I'll tell her about You! Open the door for Your message here.*

This is no ordinary thrift store. The owner has collected high-end pieces for women that she sells so inexpensively I can hardly believe it. I notice a beautiful spring jacket of bright colors from Chico's for $12.00 in exactly my size. *Are you sure?* I ask the owner. *Are you sure?*

I felt chosen and treasured as I stood there and dug into my purse for money. I asked the owner her name and a little about her life. I began to see her as a chosen daughter, a treasured soul. I had a feeling I would return to this thrift store again and again. She showed me the room where she sleeps at night—a precious apartment with a bed and a sink and a small couch, all tucked away in the back of the store. I let her talk about her life. I wanted to become the chosen priest to bless her and lead her into a new kingdom. In my mind, I'm pronouncing blessing over her life.

But I looked out the window as we finished my transaction. The snow fell harder around that tiny thrift store, so I wanted to leave quickly to drive back to my warm home before the snow accumulated too much. I would return another day after the snow melted.

By the door, I nearly tripped over a table I hadn't seen before. It held a collection of perfumes and makeup. *So strange for a thrift store*, I thought. I stopped and furrowed my brow in confusion and then wonder.

A brand-new bottle of Trish McEvoy's Blackberry Vanilla Musk shimmered right there. And beside it sat two bottles of Advanced Night Repair serum. I whipped my head back to the owner.

How could these be here? Where did you get these? The owner didn't know. Someone donated them, but she didn't have more information. She sold them to me—for next to nothing—and sent me off into the snow that bit my cheeks just like that same walk I took in my neighborhood when I felt rejected and overlooked.

But I could hardly remember those feelings as I stood there with snow falling all around me like a heavenly shaking of powdered sugar.

I held the perfume to my chest and giggled. I called my sister to tell her, and I texted her a picture I took of the perfume bottle and the face serum. I told her the story of how I was thinking of those three glamorous things—the jacket, the perfume, and even the face serum—and how they were all there in the store. "I'm so chosen and treasured!" I said, and she marveled with me.

———✺———

I remembered that scared young girl sitting with her big sister in the coffee shop and all those tears shed because she felt she would never be God's chosen.

I didn't think He loved me. He wouldn't choose *me*.

But He did.

And He saw me there in the thrift store. He didn't have to create such a lavish display of provision—of things I wanted but didn't need—but He did. After all, He chose me as His treasured possession.

He chose me.

And He chose you.

Together, we can step into the life we've been missing all this time. I don't know where we're going or what's going to happen. I offer you no clear plans. I don't know the what or the where, but I do know the *who*.

Jesus is here—choosing us, loving us, leading us step by step. We don't need to fear rejection, live in confusion, or wonder if we've missed out on the life meant for us.

This is our chosen life, and we are His chosen ones forever. One day, we'll say what Elizabeth Prentiss felt when she wrote all those years ago in a journal that might seem much like your own prayer journal. She writes, "As it is, He has led me on, step by step, answering my prayers in His own way; and I cannot bear to have a single human being doubt that it has been a perfect way. I love and adore it just as it is."[4]

I pray you embrace the God who chose you for Christ and this beautiful chosen life He's given you.

YOUR NEXT STEP

Read Colossians 1:9–14.

1. Write a description of a "day in the life" of a chosen person. How does she behave? How does she feel?

2. Which invitation to a chosen life most excites you?

3. Write out a sentence describing your new purpose as a chosen person.

4. As you trust God with your chosen life, what will you say the next time you feel rejected or confused about your calling?

ACKNOWLEDGMENTS

I once again thank my family—my "people"—far and wide who help me inhabit the reality that I'm chosen, especially my husband, Ashley, and my daughters, Sarah and Kate. I thank my parents, Brad and Linda Brown and my father-in-law and mother-in-law Curtis and Kitty Holleman. Special thanks to Jane Crandell—my new grandmother—and all the friends at the State College Alliance Church. Thank you to the theologians in my life who gave me the courage to write about being "chosen" and my teachers within Cru and beyond. Special thanks to all the women's ministry directors I've met these last few years who serve tirelessly with their extraordinary teams to help women love Jesus more. For my friends here in my neighborhood—and especially Jennifer, JoAnn, Faith, Denise, Andrea (the original Italian Mama), Deb, Sandy, and Heather—thank you for your friendship and support all these years. Thank you to Don Jacobson and the team at Moody Publishers—especially Janis Todd, Ashley Torres, and Pam Pugh—who bless me with their wisdom. I offer special thanks to Melissa Brown Kish for all those notecards she wrote with Bible verses on them for me when I didn't feel chosen and for Crystal Summers's phone calls to remind me I'm chosen. Most of all, thank you to Judy Dunagan, the one who chose my first book. I am forever thankful.

NOTES

Chapter 1: When Will I Feel Chosen?

1. Nicholas Evans, *The Horse Whisperer* (New York: Random House, 1995), 295. The movie adaptation also offers a powerful dramatization of the scene between Grace and her mother. See *The Horse Whisperer*, film, dir. Robert Redford, perf. Scarlett Johansson and Kristin Scott Thomas (Touchstone Pictures, 1998).

2. See Exodus 19:5; Deuteronomy 7:6; 14:2; 26:18; Malachi 3:17. Here we see the repetition of God claiming we are "chosen to be his treasured possession."

Chapter 2: This Life Now

1. Kay Arthur, *Lord, I Want to Know You* (Sisters, OR: Multnomah Books, 1992), 28.

2. Corrie ten Boom, *The Hiding Place* (Grand Rapids: Baker Publishing, 2006), 12.

3. Os Guinness, *The Call: Finding and Fulfilling the Central Purpose of Your Life* (Nashville: Thomas Nelson, 2003), 25.

Chapter 3: The Best Question

1. Author Becky Harling takes a look at this question in *Who Do You Say That I AM? A Fresh Encounter for Deeper Faith* (Chicago: Moody, 2018).

Chapter 4: For a Person, Not a Plan

1. See Colossians 1:16 and the explanation in *Thayer's Greek Lexicon* https://www.blueletterbible.org/lang/lexicon/lexicon.cfm?Strongs=G1519&t=NIV.

2. Coyne Stephen Sanders and Tom Gilbert, *Desilu: The Story of Lucille Ball and Desi Arnaz* (Quill, an imprint of William Morrow and Company: New York, 1993), 69.

3. *I Love Lucy*, "Lucy Goes to the Hospital," Season 2, Episode 16, Dir. William Asher, CBS, January 19, 1953.

4. A. W. Tozer, *Warfare of the Spirit: Religious Ritual Versus the Presence of the Indwelling Christ* (Chicago: Moody, 2006), 97.

5. Father Jacques Philippe, *Searching for and Maintaining Peace: A Small Treatise on Peace of Heart,* trans. George and Jannic Driscoll (New York: Alba House, 2002).

6. Paul David Tripp, *New Morning Mercies: A Daily Gospel Devotional* (Wheaton, IL: Crossway, 2014), January 1 entry.

Chapter 5: The First Invitation: Worship

1. Oprah Winfrey, *What I Know for Sure* (New York: Flatiron Books, 2014).

2. A. W. Tozer, *The Purpose of Man: Designed to Worship* (Minneapolis: Bethany, 2009), 34.

3. Ibid., 15.

4. Ibid., 71.

5. Wayne Grudem, *Systematic Theology: An Introduction to Biblical Doctrine* (Keicester: InterVarsity and Grand Rapids: Zondervan, 1994), 1003–4.

6. Matt Redman, *The Unquenchable Worshipper: Coming Back to the Heart of Worship* (Ventura: Regal, 2001), 24.

7. Grudem, 1008.

8. Elisabeth Elliot, *Keep a Quiet Heart* (Ann Arbor: Servant Publications, 2004), 20. I've also heard this quoted as "The secret of joy is Christ in me, not me in a different set of circumstances."

9. E. B. White, *Charlotte's Web*, 1952 (New York: HarperCollins, 2012), 80.

Chapter 6: The Second Invitation: Live as God's Treasured Possession

1. Oliver Gillie, "Crown Jewels Are Returned to the Public Spotlight," *Independent,* March 24, 1994. http://www.independent.co.uk/news/uk/crown-jewels-are-returned-to-the-public-spotlight-1431165.html.

2. Goppian Museum Workshop, "Permanent Museum Installations" (PDF, 2011), 9–10. http://www.goppion.com/files/pdf-download/installPMI_ENG-low.pdf.

Chapter 7: The Third Invitation: Belong to a New Family

1. Email to the author, March 30, 2017. Used with permission.

2. Tim Keller, *The Prodigal God: Recovering the Heart of the Christian Faith* (New York: Penguin, 2008), 141.

3. C. S. Lewis, *The Four Loves*, 1960 (New York: HarperCollins, 2017), 78.

4. Keller, 141.

Chapter 8: The Fourth Invitation: Complete Good Works

1. Trésor by Lancôme, described at https://www.lancome-usa.com/fragrance/collection/tresor/tresor/072025.html.

2. Story shared with permission.

3. Neil Anderson, *Victory Over the Darkness* (Minneapolis: Bethany House Publishers, 2000), 133.

4. Hannah Whitall Smith, *God Is Enough*, ed. Melvin E. Dieter and Hallie A. Dieter (Grand Rapids: Francis Asbury Press, 1986), 160.

Chapter 10: The Sixth Invitation: Become Like Jesus

1. Elizabeth Prentiss, *Stepping Heavenward, 1869* (Uhrichsville, OH: Barbour, 1998), 275.

2. Richard Foster, "Becoming Like Christ," *Christianity Today* (February 5, 1996) http://www.christianitytoday.com/ct/1996/february5/6t2026.html.

3. The 2005 Time 100: The Lives and Ideas of the World's Most Influential People, in the entry by Billy Graham, "Heroes and Icons: John Stott," *Time* (April 18, 2005), http://content.time.com/time/specials/packages/article/0,28804,1972656_1972717_1974108,00.html.

4. John Stott, "Becoming More Like Christ," sermon delivered at the Keswick Convention, July 17, 2007. Read the text of this sermon at http://www.cslewisinstitute.org/Becoming_More_Like_Christ_Stott.

5. Charles Spurgeon, "Christ's People: Imitators of Him," 1855. https://archive.spurgeon.org/sermons/0021.php.

Chapter 11: The Seventh Invitation: Live Differently from the World

1. A. W. Tozer, *The Crucified Life: How to Live a Deeper Christian Experience* (Grand Rapids: Bethany House Publishers, 2011), 41.

2. Read more about Dr. Bill Bright on his memorial page: https://www.cru.org/us/en/about/billbright/profile.html

3. Mark Bubeck, *The Adversary: The Christian Versus Demon Activity* (Chicago: Moody, 2016), 61.

Chapter 12: A Daily Consecration

1. Charles Spurgeon, "The Consecration of Priests," No. 1203, *A Sermon Delivered on the Lord's Day Morning, November 15, 1874* at the Metropolitan Tabernacle, Newington. See full text at http://www.spurgeongems.org/vols19-21/chs1203.pdf.

2. Ibid., 4.

3. Ibid., 7.

4. Ibid.

5. *The Lord of the Rings: The Fellowship of the Rings*, film, dir. Peter Jackson, perf. Liv Tyler and Elijah Wood (New Line Cinema, 2001). Watch clip on YouTube here: https://www.youtube.com/watch?v=3qPKRzyFGog.

6. Andrew Murray, *Abide in Christ*, 1888 (Apollo, PA: Ichthus Publications, 2014), 77.

Chapter 13: A New Calling and Purpose

1. Elizabeth Prentiss, *Stepping Heavenward*, 1869 (Uhrichsville: Barbour, 1998), 246.

2. Walter Henrichsen, *Disciples Are Made Not Born: Helping Others Grow to Maturity in Christ* (Colorado Springs: David C. Cook, 2011), 13.

3. Ibid.

4. Prentiss, 323.

LIVING FREELY IN A
CULTURE OF COMPARISON

KNOWING THE GOD WHO
RESCUES AND KEEPS US

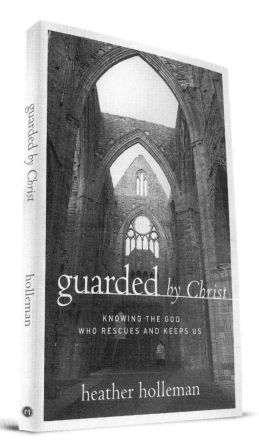

In this book, Heather Holleman explores the practical side of the radical truth that we are guarded by Christ. Follow her through a series of mental shifts—from anxiety, despair, self-importance, and self-effort—to the peace, strength, and joy that is ours in the Lord, in whatever season.

978-0-8024-1487-8 | also available as an eBook

A NEW KIND OF BIBLE STUDY...

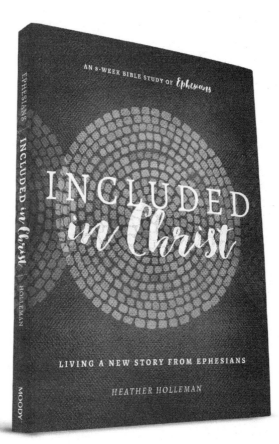